The Supportive Learning Environment

Effective Teaching Practices

Jennifer L. Hindman

Leslie W. Grant

James H. Stronge

Routledge
Taylor & Francis Group
New York London

First published 2010 by Eye On Education

Published 2013 by Routledge
711 Third Avenue, New York, NY 10017, USA
2 Park Square, Milton Park, Abingdon, Oxon OX14 4RN

Routledge is an imprint of the Taylor & Francis Group, an informa business

Library of Congress Cataloging-in-Publication Data

Hindman, Jennifer L., 1971-

   The supportive learning environment : effective teaching practices / Jennifer L. Hindman, Leslie W. Grant, James H. Stronge.
      p. cm.
   ISBN 978-1-59667-142-3
   1. Learning, Psychology of. 2. Effective teaching. 3. Cognitive styles in children. 4. Competency-based educational tests. I. Grant, Leslie W., 1968- II. Stronge, James H. III. Title.
   LB1060.H56 2010
   371.102—dc22
                                                                                          2009043003

ISBN: 978-1-596-67142-3 (pbk)

Dedication

This book is dedicated to

Teachers and administrators who seek to use their gifts for
working with children and youth in meaningful ways.

Aunt Gail who, for many years, effectively taught students when
their regularly assigned teacher could not be there, and her
daughter-in-law Liz Jarvis who is a second year teacher.

JLH

To Haddon and Eleanor, may they learn and grow through
positive environments created by classroom teachers.

LWG

My first teacher, my mother, who taught me to read.

JHS

About the Authors

Jennifer L. Hindman is an education consultant and writer who works part time at the College of William and Mary's School Leadership Institute for the School University Research Network (SURN). SURN is composed of 27 school systems working in partnership with The College of William and Mary on research and professional development initiatives. Her passion is making learning relevant as she connects the tacit knowledge with the research base. She is the coauthor of *People First: The School Leader's Guide to Building and Cultivating Relationships with Teachers* (Eye On Education, 2009), *The Teacher Quality Index: A Protocol for Teacher Selection* (ASCD, 2006) and *Handbook for Qualities of Effective Teachers* (ASCD, 2004). She has been published in numerous state and national journals, including the *Journal of Personnel Evaluation in Education, Principal Leadership,* and *Educational Leadership.* She is the former editor of *The Teacher Quality Digest.* She consults in the areas of teacher selection and effective teaching.

Jennifer has been a teacher and science specialist. She earned her doctorate in educational policy, planning, and leadership from The College of William and Mary. She can be reached at jhindman@teacherqualityresources.com.

Leslie W. Grant serves as a Visiting Assistant Professor in the School of Education at The College of William and Mary where she teaches in the teacher preparation and leadership preparation programs. Leslie is the coauthor of *Student Achievement Goal Setting: Using Data to Improve Teaching and Learning* (Eye On Education, 2009), *Teacher-made Assessments: How to Connect Curriculum, Instruction, and Student Learning* (Eye On Education, 2008), and she is the contributing author to *Qualities of Effective Teachers* (2nd ed.) authored by James H. Stronge and published by the Association for Supervision and Curriculum Development. Leslie provides consulting services in the area of classroom assessment and effective teaching.

Leslie has been a teacher, an instructional leader, and a content editor/item writer for a major test publishing company. She earned her doctoral degree in educational policy, planning, and leadership from the College of William and Mary. She can be reached at grant_leslie@cox.net.

James H. Stronge is Heritage Professor in the Educational Policy, Planning, and Leadership Area at the College of William and Mary in Williamsburg, Virginia. Among his primary research interests are teacher effective and student success, and teacher and administrator performance evaluation. He has worked with numerous school districts, state, and national educational organizations to design and develop evaluation systems for teachers, administrators, superintendents, and support personnel. He is the author or coauthor of 19 books and approximately 90 articles and technical reports on teacher quality, performance evaluation, and related issues. Selected authored, coauthored, and edited books include:

- *Student Achievement Goal Setting: Using Data to Improve Teaching and Learning* (Eye On Education, 2009)

- *Qualities of Effective Principals* (Association for Supervision and Curriculum Development, 2008)

- *Qualities of Effective Teaching, 2nd ed.* (Association for Supervision and Curriculum Development, 2007)

- *Handbook on Educational Specialist Evaluation* (Eye On Education, 2003)

- *Superintendent Evaluation Handbook* (Scarecrow Press, 2003)

- *Handbook on Teacher Evaluation* (Eye On Education, 2003)

- *Handbook on Teacher Portfolios for Evaluation and Professional Development* (Eye On Education, 2000)

His doctorate in the area of educational administration and planning was received from the University of Alabama. He has been a teacher, counselor, and district-level administrator. He can be contacted at: The College of William and Mary, School of Education, PO Box 8795, Williamsburg, VA 23187–8795; 757–221–2339; or jhstro@wm.edu.

Acknowledgements

This book and its companion book, *Planning, Instruction, and Assessment: Effective Teaching Practices* (Eye on Education, 2010) are the result of many workshops, studies, articles, and conversations with many individuals. Throughout the years, we have met many teachers, researchers, and administrators. Our interactions with them helped us to connect research to practice and sometimes inspired by the magic of a professional work from practice to research. Thank you to each of you, too numerous to acknowledge by name, who have impacted on our work.

The nexus of much of this work is coauthor James Stronge. He is like a Roman arch. His work facilitates the transportation of ideas much like the arches supported the aqueducts built centuries ago to carry water into the cities. Those who are privileged to interact with him can walk through the arch or benefit from the support of the arch. Over the years, James has involved us in effective teacher research and writing. As such our research interests in assessment, evaluation, and teacher selection have benefited from the collaboration.

We gratefully acknowledge the subscribers to the *Teacher Quality Digest* (a publication we self-published for three years) who supported our work to delve in deeply to topics related to effective teachers. Their confidence in us, inspired us, pushed us, and motivated us to identify relevant research and topics that represented a mix of the expected and the unexpected.

We would like to thank Mary Vause, a freelance copyeditor and graduate student in The College of William and Mary's School of Education. Mary completed her Master's in Education and is now a teacher. We benefited from her editorial suggestions offered before the book was ever submitted to Eye On Education.

Also, we would like to acknowledge our colleague at The College of William and Mary, Christopher Gareis, Ed.D., as a contributing author for his work on the mentoring section found in Chapter 3.

Furthermore, the efforts of the reviewers, editors, and support staff who carried this manuscript from the down the field achieving first down "milestones" to score a touchdown are commended.

Finally, we deeply appreciate Bob Sickles' commitment to recognizing the potential that a book has to contribute to the profession and his support to bring a book from author's conception to publisher's birth.

Free Downloads

Many of the tools discussed and displayed in this book are also available on the Routledge website as Adobe Acrobat files. Permission has been granted to purchasers of this book to download these tools and print them.

You can access these downloads by visiting www.routledge.com/9781596671423 and click on the Free Downloads tab.

List of Free Downloads

Contents

Part I
Research and
Practice Intertwine

1

Introduction

If you needed a dresser for your bedroom, what would you look for? After all, there are millions of dressers in the world. What would be your priorities (e.g., price, style, craftsmanship, availability)? I look for hallmarks of quality in the craftsmanship such as solid wood, dovetail drawers, butterfly joints, hand sanding, and protective finishes that allow the beauty of the wood seen. Of course I want it all and at a good price. However, my funds are limited and so I make choices. There is one dresser in my home that I'd like to tell you about, it was my husband's childhood dresser that his mother picked up at a garage sale. Over the years, I have changed how the dresser looks and functions in response to my household needs. I refinished the top to let the natural wood show, painted the body of the dresser twice, and changed out the drawer pulls a few times. This dresser was mass produced with dovetailed joints, and with my attention, it has become a piece that has functioned well in each setting.

To a degree, teachers are like dressers, there are 3.9 million teachers in the United States a number expected to grow to 4.4 million by 2016.[1] There is a lot of variation in the effectiveness teachers, influenced by personal attributes, acquired knowledge, and learned skills. Decades of research abounds on qualities of effective teachers. There are some teachers who are like finely crafted dressers in that there are numerous hallmarks of quality from how they interact with people to the learning outcomes recorded. On the other end, there are the ineffective teachers whose instruction barely holds together like a flimsy cardboard backed dresser. Many teachers, however, are like my husband's dresser—they are effective, and if not quite effective, can be made so with some targeted efforts. Even better, these teachers can make choices to be even better like I enhanced the fit and usefulness of dresser. In this book, *The Supportive Learning Environment: Effective Teaching Practices*, both elements of finely crafted classrooms are explored and the background attributes of the teachers who created them—in essence, how teachers create environments and relationships that inspire and motivate students. The companion book,

Planning, Instruction, and Assessment: Effective Teaching Practices, addresses the planning, instructional, and assessment choices that teachers make to construct learning experiences. Both books provide tools for practitioners to use to hone their craft.

In *Student Achievement Goal Setting: Using Data to Improve Teaching and Learning* (Eye On Education, 2009), we asked the critical question "Why do we have schools?" at the beginning of the book. In answer we offered "…there are only two reasons why schooling exists: (1) teaching and learning, and (2) supporting teaching and learning."[2] It is this latter reason—supporting teaching and learning—that is the focus of *The Supportive Learning Environment: Effective Teaching Practices.* In particular, we address the following questions related to how and why we can and should provide proper support mechanisms for teachers and students.

- ◆ What is teacher effectiveness?
- ◆ Why is teacher quality important?
- ◆ What is the relationship between teacher quality and student learning?
- ◆ How is the book organized?
- ◆ How can the book be used to promote teacher quality?

What Is Teacher Effectiveness?[a]

Teacher effectiveness is a broad concept[3] that can be defined in many ways.[4] The word "quality" denotes the experience of being with a special teacher, and the term "effectiveness" works well when referring to analytical evidence. We choose to use the terms "quality" and "effectiveness" interchangeably. One clear and undeniable way to define teacher quality is to personally know an effective teacher, or to have benefited from the tutelage and teaching of an extraordinary teacher. Another way to define teacher effectiveness is to analyze—or dissect—it based on the extant research about what makes teachers effective. In this section, we briefly explore both perspectives: *analyzing* a quality teacher and *interacting* with a quality teacher.

Although we may not be able to define teacher quality with precision, we certainly can identify key teacher qualities that form the foundation of any useful definition. Studies examining effective teacher characteristics are profuse and often seem to seek an elusive secret formula for teacher quality. Unfortunately, there is no single magic elixir for quality teaching. However, one thing we know for certain about teacher quality is that it is multi-dimensional and these multiple dimensions interact to form the chemistry of what makes good teachers good.

Figure 1.1 notes some key components of a quality teacher.[b]

---

a This section of the chapter is replicated in Chapter 1 of the Eye On Education companion book, *Planning, Instruction, and Assessment: Effective Teaching Practices* (2010).

b For a more comprehensive review and discussion of key teacher dispositions, skills, and knowledge, see: Stronge, J. H. (2007). *Qualities of effective teachers* (2nd ed.). Alexandria, VA: Association for Supervision and Curriculum Development.

Figure 1.1. Selected Characteristics of Quality Teachers

♦ *Communication skills* including the ability to listen to and value what students have to say;[5]

♦ *Teacher preparation* in terms of content knowledge[6] and certification,[7] among others;

♦ *Personal dispositions* such as enthusiasm, motivation, and reflectivity;[8]

♦ *Personal relationships* with students built on fairness, trust, and respectfulness;[9]

♦ *Classroom management* that provides a safe, robust, disciplined, and vibrant learning environment;[10]

♦ *Instructional planning, delivery, and ongoing student assessment* combined in such a way as to constantly monitor and deliver differentiated, effective instruction;[11] and

♦ Clearly focused goals and high expectations to promote student achievement.[12]

Why Is Teacher Quality Important?

Regardless of how we choose to define quality, building-level administrators and teachers know that the work of good teachers results in improvements for students, including improved instructional opportunities and improved student learning. Although we highlighted a number of key dispositions and practices (i.e., teaching processes) in the section above, let's consider the impact (i.e., results) of a high-quality teacher:

♦ Fewer discipline issues;

♦ Better relationships with their students; and, most importantly,

♦ Higher student achievement results.[13]

Thus, any worthy definition should take into account both the *process* of teaching (e.g., quality instructional delivery skills) and the *results* of teaching (e.g., student achievement gains).

So why does teacher quality matter? Because learning matters. If we hope for our children a better quality education and a brighter tomorrow, we also must hope for—and support in every practical way—quality teachers.

What Is the Relationship Between Teacher Quality and Student Learning?[c]

Analyses of data from teacher value-added assessment studies[14] offer compelling evidence regarding the influence of the classroom teacher on student learning.[15] The overarching finding from value-added studies is that effective teachers are, indeed, essential for student success. In fact, it has been estimated that out of all the factors that

---

c This section of the chapter is replicated in Chapter 1 of the Eye On Education companion book, *Planning, Instruction, and Assessment: Effective Teaching Practices* (2010).

are within the control of schools, teachers have the greatest impact on student achievement.[16] Consider the following specific findings presented in Figure 1.2.

Figure 1.2. Teacher Impact on Student Achievement

Major Findings	Study
♦ The impact of teachers is far greater than that of overall school effects. In other words, "which teacher a student gets within a school matters more than which school the student happens to attend."	Nye, Konstantopoulos, & Hedges, 2004
♦ Beginning in third grade, children placed with highly effective teachers scored on average at the 96th percentile on Tennessee's mathematics state assessment, whereas children placed with ineffective teachers scored on average at the 42nd percentile.	Wright, Horn, & Sanders, 1997
♦ Students of less-effective teachers experienced reading achievement gains of one-third standard deviation less than students with effective teachers.	Nye, Konstantopoulos, & Hedges, 2004
♦ Students of less-effective teachers experienced mathematics achievement gains of almost one-half standard deviation less than students with effective teachers.	Nye, Konstantopoulos, & Hedges, 2004
♦ Lower-achieving students are more likely to be placed with less-effective teachers.	Wright, Horn, & Sanders, 1997
♦ If a student had a high-performing teacher for just one year, the student likely would remain ahead of peers for at least the next few years of schooling (residual effect).	Mendro, 1998
♦ Third grade students of teachers in the top quartile of effectiveness (based on hierarchical linear modeling predictions) scored approximately 30 to 40 scaled score points higher than expected on the Virginia Standards of Learning state assessment in English, Mathematics, Science, and Social Studies, respectively. Students of teachers in the bottom quartile of effectiveness scored approximately 24 to 32 points below expected scores.	Stronge, Tucker, & Ward, 2003
♦ The teacher has a larger effect on student achievement than any other school-related factor, including class size and ability levels within a class.	Wright, Horn, & Sanders, 1997
♦ Fifth grade students scored approximately 30 percentile points higher in both reading and mathematics in one year when assigned to top-quartile teachers as compared to those students assigned to bottom-quartile teachers.	Stronge, Ward, & Grant, 2008

To summarize the impact of effective teachers on student learning, Wright, Horn, and Sanders surmised that "seemingly more can be done to improve education by improving the effectiveness of teachers than by any other single factor."[17] Yes, we do need *highly qualified teachers* as required in the U.S. federal legislation *No Child Left Behind*. However, much more importantly, we need *high-quality teachers*.

How Is the Book Organized?

The following are premises of *The Supportive Learning Environment: Effective Teaching Practices*:

♦ Teachers come to the profession with dispositions nurtured by parents, mentors, teachers, and life experiences (Chapter 2).

♦ Teachers seek and acquire knowledge to become effective teachers and then further develop their professional knowledge and skills (Chapter 3).

♦ Teachers use these dispositions and knowledge to create a positive, robust classroom environment that nurtures learners (Chapter 4).

♦ Teachers take advantage of support mechanisms and integrate those supportive skills into their teaching repertoire in order to become masterful teachers (Chapter 5).

The Venn diagram (Figure 1.3) below depicts how *The Supportive Learning Environment: Effective Teaching Practices* and its companion book, *Planning, Instruction, and Assessment: Effective Teaching Practices* (Eye On Education, 2010), address the extant research related to teacher quality.

Figure 1.3. The Relationship Between the Companion Effective Practices Books

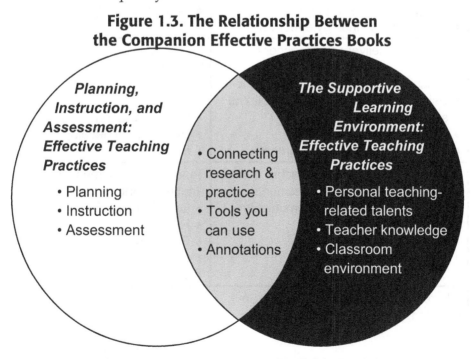

The book focuses on research-based practices of teacher quality. Three parts comprise each book, they are:

♦ *Part I* focuses on selected key elements that support teaching and learning, namely, teachers' personal dispositions, professional development, and the importance of creating and sustaining a positive learning environment (Chapters 1 to 5).

♦ *Part II* offers reproducible resources for use by teachers and those working with teachers.

♦ *Part III* includes an annotated bibliography of key publications that are related to supporting teacher quality.

Figure 1.4 summarizes the relationship between the two books as they address essential elements for teacher quality.

Figure 1.4. Overview of Content for the Companion Books

Chapter	*Planning, Instruction, and Assessment: Effective Teaching Practices*	*The Supportive Learning Environment: Effective Teaching Practices*
1	♦ Teacher effectiveness defined ♦ Impact of teacher effectiveness on student achievement	♦ Teacher effectiveness defined ♦ Impact of teacher effectiveness on student achievement
2	Instructional planning and teacher quality ♦ Focusing on essential knowledge and skills ♦ Differentiating instruction ♦ Using Response-to-Intervention ♦ Integrating technology effectively	Personal dispositions of quality teachers ♦ Immediacy ♦ Credibility ♦ Caring ♦ Engaging caregivers
3	Instructional delivery and teacher effectiveness ♦ Teaching for conceptual understanding ♦ Using questioning as an instructional strategy ♦ Developing inquiring minds ♦ Increasing student engagement	Professional knowledge and teacher effectiveness ♦ Certification ♦ Experience ♦ Communication ♦ Professional development ♦ Mentoring
4	Student assessment and teacher quality ♦ Developing aligned assessments ♦ Creating rubrics that communicate expectations ♦ Providing feedback ♦ Using assessment data	Teacher management skill, classroom attributes, and teacher effectiveness ♦ Learning environment ♦ Rules ♦ Routines ♦ Student ownership ♦ Time management
5	Interrelationships among planning, instruction, and assessment	Supporting teacher quality ♦ School culture ♦ Teacher reflection ♦ High expectations

How Can the Book Be Used to Promote Teacher Quality?

Effective teachers know how to use resources around them and how to maximize their own time as well as time in the classroom. *The Supportive Learning Environment: Effective Teaching Practices*, along with its companion book, *Planning, Instruction, and Assessment: Effective Teaching Practices*, focus on elements within education that can support effective teaching and can therefore also support student learning.

Our intent is that the book will be a valuable resource for the following audiences:

♦ Teachers—including classroom teachers, resource teachers, and educators in other settings—who desire to improve their own performances and the performances of their students through this value-added methodology;

♦ Teacher leaders who are in a position to impact teacher practice through their support and expertise;

♦ Administrators who supervise and support teachers; and,

♦ Staff development specialists who plan and deliver training focused on improving instructional practices.

Regardless of your position in the enterprise of teaching and learning, it is our sincere hope that *The Supportive Learning Environment: Effective Teaching Practices* benefits your school, your teaching practices, and, most importantly, your students.

Notes

1   Occupational Outlook Handbook, 2008-09 Edition, *Teachers—Preschool, Kindergarten, Elementary, Middle, and Secondary*. Retrieved July 10, 2009 from http://www.bls.gov/oco/ocos069.htm

2   Stronge & Grant, 2009.

3   Darling-Hammond, 2008; Stronge, 2002; Stronge, 2007.

4   Yin & Kwok, 1999.

5   Darling-Hammond, 2000; Emmer, Evertson, & Anderson, 1980.

6   Felter, 1999.

7   Darling-Hammond, 2000; Darling-Hammond, Berry, & Thoreson, 2001; Goldhaber & Brewer, 2001; Hawk, Coble, & Swanson, 1985; Haycock, 2000; Miller, McKenna, & McKenna, 1998.

8   National Association of Secondary School Principals, 1997; Peart & Campbell, 1999; Stronge, 2007.

9   Marzano, Pickering, & McTighe, 1993; McBer, 2000.

10 Corbett & Wilson, 2004; Stronge, Ward, Tucker, & Hindman, 2008.

11 Marzano, 2006; Tomlinson, 1999.

12 Cotton, 2000; Johnson, 1997; Marzano et al., 1993; Mason, Schroeter, Combs, & Washington, 1992; McBer, 2000; Peart & Campbell, 1999; Shellard & Protheroe, 2000.

13 Ralph, Kesten, Lang, & Smith, 1998; Stronge, Ward, Tucker, & Hindman, 2008.

14 For an explanation and examples of teacher value-added assessment, see Tucker & Stronge, 2005.

15 See, for example, Mendro, 1998; Nye, Konstantopoulos, & Hedges, 2004; Wright, Horn, & Sanders, 1997.

16 See, for example: Carey, 2004; Leithwood, Louis, Anderson, & Wahlstrom, 2004; Stronge, Ward, Tucker, & Hindman, 2008.

17 Wright, Horn, & Sanders, 1997, p. 63.

2

What Dispositions Support Teaching and Student Learning?

For many, teaching is not a *job;* rather, it is a *vocation.* The difference between the two words reveals the different attitudes with which individual teachers view their work with children. Consider the differences between the two terms:

- A *job* is something that has to be done on a regular basis for which a person receives compensation.

- A *vocation* is a calling or a special function of an individual or group.

Job and *vocation* convey significantly different dispositions, or attitudes, toward teaching. Although all of us recognize the importance of fair and reasonable pay to attract, retain, and support good teachers, we also know that it is those teachers who view their work as a calling who are most likely to be effective in the classroom.

Students who remember exceptional teachers generally recount interesting lessons, but those anecdotes are shared in the context of how the teacher made the student feel valued, special, and important. That is, the personal connection is first and foremost. No one says, "My favorite teacher had the best bulletin boards or gave easy tests." Rather, lasting memories echo sentiments such as:

- "She treated us as adults and was always warm and affectionate…couldn't wait for those two hours to come when she taught you."[1]

- She was "interested in our social lives which other teachers would not have cared about."[2]

- He had "infinite patience and tolerance for anything except unkindness."[3]

Such fond memories are usually reciprocal. One teacher wrote of wanting his students to have powerful learning experiences to carry with them throughout their lives, such as those his own teacher had given him.[4] Another teacher told his son, "We teach for the enduring relationships we develop with students."[5] The Internet search engine Google located more than 50 million entries for searches run using the words "my best teacher" and "my favorite teacher."[6] Clearly, teachers are an important—indeed, essential—part of students' school experience.

This chapter focuses on the dispositions of the individual teacher that enhance the teacher's ability to connect with students. So, then, the answers to the question of "What dispositions support teaching and student learning?"—as posed in the title of this chapter—include the following:

- *Immediacy*—the extent to which the teacher connects with his or her students on a personal level;

- *Credibility*—the extent to which students and others in the school community trust the teacher;

- *Caring*—the extent to which students feel that the teacher cares about them; and

- *Welcoming and engaging caregivers*—the extent to which the teacher engages parents/caregivers both at school and at home.

Immediacy

What Is Immediacy?

Immediacy refers to behaviors that draw students psychologically closer to their teachers, such as eye contact, smiles, head nods, and extra communication outside of the typical classroom dialogue, such as greetings at the door and impromptu discussions of after school activities. Immediacy can open up the learner to being receptive to the teacher and "generates increased involvement and enthusiasm for the material and the instruction."[7]

Positive immediacy refers to behaviors that make teachers approachable, likeable, trustworthy, and in general psychologically "safe." For example, in one study, the simple act of saying "hello" paid dividends in terms of increased on-task student behavior. In this study of positive initial contact and on-task behavior, researchers observed three students in three different classes who had difficulty getting on-task at the start of class. Each student was observed between four and six times. An observer noted that the students exhibited on-task behaviors for the first ten minutes of class 37%, 48%, and 52% of the time, respectively. Their teachers were instructed to greet their student by using the student's name and giving a positive comment. Over a period of three to four weeks (six to eight observations), the observer noted that students' on-task behavior, after being greeted at the door, increased on average to 66%, 67%, and 87%, respectively.[8] The simple act of saying "hello" conveys the message that "I am glad you are here."

How Do Good Teachers Convey Immediacy?

Immediacy is conveyed in many different ways. Behaviors include head nodding, smiling, eye contact, story telling, calling students by name, asking for student opinions, providing feedback, and offering extra help.[9] In essence, high immediacy is like making a deposit into a bank. As the bank account grows, interest is earned, and dividends are paid. So when something unexpected occurs and an emotional withdraw is made, there is still a cushion of security. Similarly, when a teacher continues to make positive contact with students, students begin to feel that the teacher cares about them (caring is discussed in detail later in this chapter) and, thus, when an academic issue or a behavioral issue needs to be addressed, the student and the teacher have built a foundation for positive interaction.

Students' affective learning (see sidebar) is significantly influenced by teachers' high immediacy actions.[10] "Students who feel that a teacher uses immediacy behaviors are more likely to feel a positive relationship exists, and it is built on liking, encouragement, and support."[11]

> **Affective Learning Defined**
>
> Affective learning relates to the student's attitude toward the course, classroom behavior, content, and teacher.

How Can Teachers Assess Their Immediacy Behaviors?

Consider the following situation:

Dick Tate (fictional teacher) was hired to teach high school Algebra, Algebra II, and remedial math. He was a career switcher who knew mathematics, and his lesson plans revealed that he was thoughtful in how he scaffolded examples to teach concepts. From the time students came into the classroom to when they left at the end of the period, he talked about mathematics. If he had been a teacher on television, all would have been well as he taught from his script (i.e., plan). As his chalk clicked over the chalkboard, he'd ask if there were any questions. But, unfortunately, he rarely turned around or looked up to see students' raised hands. If a student called out a question, he would answer it, but he rarely looked back to visually acknowledge the student. Mr. Tate wanted to be a good teacher; he truly wanted his students to learn, yet he never connected with his students on a personal level. He did not seem to understand that teaching is not all about the content—it is about relationships and motivation.

A teacher like Mr. Tate would benefit from an analysis of his interactions with students during the class period. The template in Figure 2.1 (page 12) is an *Immediacy Interaction Record*. (A reproducible blank template of the *Immediacy Interaction Record* is available in Part II.) It is designed for a teacher like Mr. Tate who has the foundational components of good teaching but lacks an awareness of how personal interactions can complement the students' learning experience. The *Immediacy Interaction Record* can be used as a pre- and postintervention measure.

Figure 2.1. Sample Completed Immediacy Interactions Record

	Tally	Total
Verbal		
Extra help		
Feedback		
Greeting	/	/
Positive comment/compliment	/	/
Student life inquiry (e.g., sports, band, special event)		
Other—specify		
Nonverbal		
Eye contact		
Head nod	/ /	2
Positive facial expression		
Smile	/	/
Other—specify		

Immediacy Interaction Record

This tool is for the specific purpose of recording the interactions between the teacher and students. If observations, walkthroughs, and other data sources suggest that a teacher has the planning, teaching, and assessing tools and can use them, perhaps what is needed to enhance instruction is a focus on personal qualities. The *Immediacy Interaction Record* focuses on the interactions that enhance personal contact with students. Eye contact, affirming communication, head nods, and the like, are all ways by which teachers can build immediacy. For an example, look at the *Immediacy Interactions Record* for the first 20 minutes of Mr. Tate's class in Figure 2.1.

As illustrated, the *Record* is nearly blank. In the first 20 minutes of class, students came into the room and started on the warmup activity while Mr. Tate monitored the class change in the hallway. When he came into the room, the teacher took attendance while walking around the room and checked to see that homework had been completed. Then, he went over the homework and answered any questions the students had. He did greet a student who came in late with a brief smile and indicated that he was glad that she was feeling well enough to come back to school.

The Intervention

The fictional teacher clearly did not exhibit behaviors that promote immediacy. The observer already knew that although the teacher handled the instructional part of the classroom well, he failed to establish the personal connection with students before class began and during class time. Ideally, the observer would ask the teacher about his or her interactions with students during the class time that was observed. Teachers like the fictional Dick Tate often only focus on impersonal interactions in the lesson, such as "students were attending, asked me to slow down or repeat," and the like. A mentor teacher, administrator, and so on, can probe deeper about interactions between the teacher and specific students. The further probing would reveal whether the teacher was affirming the student as an individual by asking validating questions and/or using supportive nonverbal communication. Thus, the *Record* serves as an "eye opener" about the teacher's immediacy in the classroom. After reviewing the observations on the *Record*, the teacher can be encouraged to take some initial steps. Three specific steps are helpful in improving immediacy:

- *Expressions:* More receptive body language would communicate immediacy to students. Encourage Mr. Tate to relax his arms, smile more, look at students when they are answering questions, etc.

- *Greeting:* Because Mr. Tate is supposed to be at the door monitoring the hall and his classroom during class changes, he has an opportunity to say hello to students. Also, he could try to ask one or two students about their day or about a school activity, such as how a baseball player did in his game.

- *Questions:* Mr. Tate should make a concerted effort to ask students if they have any questions when he is turned around from the board and facing the class, so that he can see their hands. In the event that a student calls out a question when he is writing on the board, Mr. Tate should stop writing, turn around, look at the student, and listen. Eye contact communicates that he values the student. It also gives the student an opportunity to view facial cues. This simple action tells students that the teacher is interested in their questions.

Teacher Credibility

Why Does Teacher Credibility Matter?

Teaching is a social activity in which the learner and educator interact to form meaning. Credibility involves an assessment of a person's honesty, skill, and subject knowledge, as well as reliability (i.e., dependability). These combined factors facilitate students' belief in what the teacher says. Credibility is based on long-term and short-term experiences. The teacher-student relationship is built on credibility established at the beginning of the year and reaffirmed throughout the school year.

People judge credibility through their assessment of their interactions with the individual and on past events. Our knowledge of a situation often persuades us to accept or reject the ideas shared by someone else. Credibility may be developed over time, or it may be a quick judgment based on attire, speech patterns, nonverbal communication, and physical appearance which all contribute to credibility assessments about the teacher. When relationships have time to develop, past events are used to inform decisions on the credible nature of an individual or the organization the person represents. In short, credibility relates to how likely students believe it is that a teacher will do what he or she says.

How Does Teacher Credibility Affect Teacher Effectiveness?

Teacher credibility is a facet implicit in teacher effectiveness. Students do not trust a teacher if they do not have faith that the teacher's actions will be aligned with words. When a behavior needs to be addressed or an academic issue arises, distrust between the student and teacher may prevent resolution of the issue. Figure 2.2 reviews research studies related to credibility.

Figure 2.2. Credibility and Teacher Effectiveness

Related Findings	Citation
◆ A teacher's verbal ability is positively linked to student achievement. A teacher's credibility is tied to following through on promises and the teacher's ability to demonstrate expert knowledge through communication.	O'Brien, 2001; Darling-Hammond, 2000; Farling, Stone, & Winston, 1999
◆ At-risk students considered teachers effective when they demonstrated caring through self-disclosure and effective communication.	Peart & Campbell, 1999
◆ Students of teachers who conveyed verbal caring messages rated their teachers as more credible when the teachers also followed through with nonverbal caring messages.	Trevon & Hanson, 2004
◆ Students who perceived their teachers as competent, trustworthy, and caring found their teachers to be more credible even in a situation in which the teacher "let students down" because of an ineffective presentation.	Thweatt & McCroskey, 1998

To summarize, a teacher's effectiveness is related to the teacher's credibility. A teacher's relationship with his or her students is integral to the success for both parties as social influences come into play. For learners, new material is an unknown, and to acquire the knowledge needed to traverse the unknown, they need to rely on their teacher to create meaningful, trusting experiences for them. When a student deems a teacher credible, the relationship is strengthened and bridges to ideas and new knowledge are built.

Caring

Why Does Caring Matter?

A student will spend about 180 days out of the year in their classroom, and he or she should be better off on the 180th day than on the first day. With the emphasis on accountability to make student achievement gains, talking about an affective factor such as caring may seem out of place. In fact, research and personal experience from years as students and teachers tells us, emphatically, that teacher caring does make a difference in student outcomes.

"Effective teachers are effective people....They are warm and caring, they enjoy life, and they are enthusiastic about helping other people grow and develop."[12] For students, respect, fairness, humor, and expectations all fit under the umbrella of caring. "He cares about the students and he cares that you do well," said one high school student about his teacher. "...[H]e makes sure you do well even though he might give you a lot of work. ..."[13]

A study of adults who were considered at-risk students when they were in school found that characteristics of effective teachers include elements related to caring. Effective teachers are: clear communicators, positive motivators, and unbiased individuals.[14] An at-risk student aptly surmised that the best thing for a teacher to do is "to care...to understand. You've got to go beyond the boundaries of what you're supposed to do as a teacher to help the person learn. Because if not, the kid will say, 'Oh they're giving up on me, so I might as well give up on myself.'"[15]

Every day good teachers build relationships and demonstrate caring with their students. They think about both their students' academic performance and about them as individuals. They ask students about their lives and what is occurring. They also do the following:

♦ Seek to understand their students' community and cultures.[16]

♦ Invest time getting to know students as individuals in addition to working with them.[17]

♦ Encourage their students to meet high expectations.[18]

♦ Care deeply about their students.[19]

How Do Students, Teachers, and Researchers View the Impact of Caring?

Caring is an element that is often thought of as an intangible disposition. However, by asking students and teachers and through research of caring teachers, the outward, tangible characteristics of caring can come to light. Figure 2.3 describes how each group describes the caring teacher.

Figure 2.3. Views on the Caring Teacher

Students believe that caring teachers...[20]	Caring *teachers* believe that...[21]	*Researchers* have found that caring teachers...[22]
♦ Have a caring relationship with students ♦ Are committed to students ♦ Are sensitive to student needs ♦ Model a "caring" attitude toward their own work ♦ Provide constructive feedback ♦ Demonstrate concern and empathy ♦ Respect students as individuals ♦ Care about student academic success ♦ Show respect for students and student differences	♦ Every student has the right to a caring and competent teacher ♦ Confidentiality must be respected between teacher and student ♦ Caring and learning are equally important to educating children ♦ Their love for children is a key to their success	♦ Are committed to students ♦ Have beliefs that affirm the value of the whole child and his or her ethnic and cultural background ♦ Desire to constantly grow ♦ Share who they are with students ♦ Know their students ♦ Establish relationships with their students ♦ Respect and cultivate students' talents ♦ Focus on growth and development of students ♦ Form relationships with students and colleagues based on respect

What Does the Research Say About the Connection Between Teacher Caring and Student Achievement?

Studies support the link between caring and student achievement as well as a host of other factors, such as effort and motivation. Figure 2.4 provides a review of research findings regarding the connection between caring and factors affecting student achievement.

In summary, the caring teacher can impact academic achievement as well as effort and motivation, which are factors related to student achievement. Caring, as noted by the last two research studies noted in Figure 2.4, involves much more than attending to affective needs. It also means providing support for meeting academic needs as well. Teachers combine caring and high academic expectations to create the ultimate recipe for success. For example, Janet Gannon, a fifth and sixth grade teacher, models caring in the expectations that she developed for her students. The expectations are:

♦ *Think before you talk.* Consider the range of actions that can be taken, depending on the word choice, so students feel safe and secure in the classroom environment.

♦ *Do your best work.* Make goals to improve professional practice so that students see the teacher modeling the common refrain in classrooms to "do your best."

Figure 2.4. Related Findings and Teacher Caring

Related Findings	Citation
♦ A school saw improvements in attendance, promotion rates, grades, and graduation rates when teachers began to communicate caring through simple actions such as walking around the room, calling students, tutoring students, and reaching out to families. "Students aim higher—and are more likely to reach their goals—when teachers value them" (p. 44).	Sternberg, 2005
♦ A study that used data from the National Educational Longitudinal Study of 1988 revealed that student perceptions regarding teachers' rapport, instructional quality, feedback, and respect for students had a significant effect on academic achievement.	Adams & Singh, 1998
♦ In a longitudinal study of 248 students, perceived caring by teachers was significantly and positively related to the social responsibility goals of students and to student academic effort, regardless of race or family background. Descriptions of caring teachers mirrored descriptions of effective parents, with students internalizing the goals and values stressed in school.	Wentzel, 1997
♦ Interviews of high school drop-outs revealed that students characterized their best teachers as caring individuals who took the time to give extra help. Conversely, the worst teachers were those who lacked patience and were described as "mean." The researchers concluded that caring was a main discriminator for teachers.	Engle, 1994
♦ Students associate caring actions differently depending upon achievement levels. High-achieving learners indicate that help on academic issues is an indicator of caring. Low-achieving students identified personality-related factors as indicators of caring. Both groups noted the importance of knowing students as individuals.	Hoy & Weinstein, 2006
♦ Teachers who build relationships with students and construct learning experiences to meet students' needs have students who will work harder for them.	Crabtree, 2004
♦ College-aged study participants indicated that caring/empathetic was the most important quality of a teacher followed by patient (#2), friendly (#3), interesting (#4), and good teaching skills/ability (#5). Examination of negative characteristics of teachers found that seven of ten (e.g., boring, inconsiderate) were related to relationships.	Nikitina & Furoka, 2009

♦ *Tell them why.* Think about and communicate the purpose behind actions. This does not mean rationalizing to students every instructional detail. Rather, if students ask something as common as, "Why do we have to do this?" there is a solid and valid response.

♦ *Help them experience success.* Design lessons that use strategies that enable students to experience success.[23]

How Can Data Be Collected About the Caring Teacher?

Caring, as discussed previously, is an intangible characteristic which manifests itself in tangible ways, often through interactions among people. Teachers and students have hundreds of interactions each day—some lasting a mere second. Depending on the teacher-student relationship, interactions may be positive/strained, formal/informal, respectful/disrespectful, and a host of other descriptors. How do teachers show they care during the school day? What gives commonplace interactions that "caring spin"?

Observing Teacher-to-Student Interactions

The Nature of Teacher-to-Student Interactions Form (Figure 2.5) focuses on the teacher's behavior towards students. (A reproducible blank template of the *Teacher-to-Student Interactions Form* is available in Part II.) An observer watches the teacher and notes two items for each interaction. The first is the purpose for the interaction, which may be behavior management, instruction, feedback, or other factors. The second is the type of the interaction, which may be verbal or nonverbal. The tone is classified as positive, neutral, or negative.

Focusing on Number of Interactions

Teacher–student interactions occur constantly. The form has space for thirty interactions and provides a sampling of how the teacher interacts with students. The observation length varies based on the classroom activity. For example, if a teacher is doing a rapid-fire-type review with questions and answers, thirty interactions will take around five minutes and will be mostly instructional in nature. More likely, the observation will be conducted during an instructional period that is teacher-directed instruction or during a teacher-facilitated student work time. In these situations, the observation takes approximately fifteen minutes. Note that the form could be modified to record interactions using a given time interval.

Watching the Teacher

The teachers' actions influence how students perceive caring messages from their teachers. This form does not examine the students' response to the interaction nor does it query students about teacher caring. It is not realistic for a single observer to watch both the teacher and the students as interactions will be missed. Think of how an effective teacher handles an inattentive student while teaching. The teacher may not say a word, but rather continue teaching while moving to stand beside the student or perhaps give the student a "knowing look." By observing just the teacher, an observer can note

Figure 2.5. Sample Nature of Teacher-to-Student Interaction Form

Nature of Teacher-to-Student Interactions

Teacher: _____ Number of Students: _____

Observation Date: _____ Start Time: _____ End Time: _____

Directions: Focus on the teacher's interactions with students. For each observed interaction, make two checkmarks, one to indicate the purpose for the interaction and the second to describe the tone of the interaction as positive, neutral, or negative. Then tally the number interactions related to behavior management and tone. Suggested observation is for 30 interactions. This is approximately 15 minutes.

KEY	
B when the purpose of the interaction is for Behavior Management	+ indicates positive/affirming/praise
I when the purpose of the interaction is for Instruction	N indicates neutral
F when the purpose of the interaction is for Feedback	- indicates negative/punitive
O is for "Other" which should be specified	

#		#	
1	Purpose: ☐ B ☒ I ☐ F ☐ O Tone: ☐ + ☒ N ☐ -	16	Purpose: ☐ B ☐ I ☐ F ☐ O Tone: ☐ + ☐ N ☐ -
2	Purpose: ☒ B ☐ I ☐ F ☐ O Tone: ☐ + ☒ N ☐ -		Purpose: ☐ B ☐ I ☐ F ☐ O
3	Purpose: ☐ B ☐ I ☐ F ☒ O Tone: ☐ + ☐ N ☐ -		
4	Purpose: ☐ B ☐ I ☐ F ☐ O Tone: ☐ + ☐ N ☐ -		Purpose: ☐ B ☐ I ☐ F ☐ O Tone: ☐ + ☐ N ☐ -
5	Purpose: ☐ I ☐ F ☐ O ☐ N ☐ -	20	Purpose: ☐ B ☐ I ☐ F ☐ O Tone: ☐ + ☐ N ☐ -
6		21	Purpose: ☐ B ☐ I ☐ F ☐ O Tone: ☐ + ☐ N ☐ -
7			Purpose: ☐ B ☐ I ☐ F ☐ O Tone: ☐ + ☐ N ☐ -
8			Purpose: ☐ B ☐ I ☐ F ☐ O Tone: ☐ + ☐ N ☐ -
9			Purpose: ☐ B ☐ I ☐ F ☐ O
10			
11	Tone:		
12	Purpose: ☐ B ☐ I ☐ F ☐ O Tone: ☐ + ☐ N ☐ -	27	Purpose: Tone:
13	Purpose: ☐ B ☐ I ☐ F ☐ O Tone: ☐ + ☐ N ☐ -	28	Purpose: Tone:
14	Purpose: ☐ B ☐ I ☐ F ☐ O Tone: ☐ + ☐ N ☐ -	29	Purpose: Tone:
15	Purpose: ☐ B ☐ I ☐ F ☐ O Tone: ☐ + ☐ N ☐ -	30	Purpose: ☐ -

Purpose is why the teacher and student are interacting. In the scenario, it is for "F – Feedback" on the students' essay.

Tone is more subjective.

- If the teacher asks questions to help the student make stronger arguments, then the tone is positive.
- If teacher indicates areas where improvement can be made, then the tone is neutral as the action did not positively or adversely involve the student in the process.
- If the teacher says the essay needs work and goes onto the next student, then the tone is negative. Just as if the teacher had frowned since the only message sent to the student was "this is not good."

Prior to showing the teacher the observation form, observers can ask teachers about their perceptions of the interactions. Often teachers perceive a class went well even if the interactions were primarily neutral and if behavior interactions, even negative tone ones, were effective. From a student perceptive, this is not a positive classroom environment, just simply a well-managed one.

Discussion of the Observation

Totals						
Behavior		Positive		Neutral	Negative	
Instruction		Positive		Neutral	Negative	
Feedback		Positive		Neutral	Negative	
Other		Positive		Neutral	Negative	
OVERALL		Positive		Neutral	Negative	

Comments

these more subtle interactions. If two observers are in the classroom, one can watch the teacher and the other can note the students' reactions to the interactions as effective, ineffective, or neutral. Also, an observer could spend a portion of time focusing on teacher behaviors and then shift the focus to student behaviors.

Consider a teacher providing instructional support as students are working on their persuasive essays. For this example, imagine the teacher standing beside one student's desk and skimming over the essay to offer suggestions. The form in Figure 2.5 (page 19) shows data collected regarding this interaction.

Reflecting with the Form

The *Nature of Teacher-to-Student Interactions Form* does not link specific interactions with students; rather, it seeks to establish patterns of interactions. In the "Totals" section, the observer tallies how many of each type of interaction occurred and the tone of the interaction. The "Overall" box is the sum of each type of tone from each of the four purposes. It provides the big picture of the tone of the classroom interactions during the observation period. The teacher and observer can discuss the tone associated with each type of interaction as well as the overall numbers. Positive, neutral, and negative interactions each have their place in a classroom. However, research findings suggest that students are more engaged and motivated in positive classroom environments.

Welcoming and Engaging Caregivers

Why Engage Caregivers?

The involvement of parents benefits the school and allows teachers to gain a greater understanding of students' lives, while parents meanwhile benefit by increasing their knowledge of child development.[24] (Much of the research literature addresses parents, so we use the term *parent* along with the more inclusive term *caregiver* to recognize the adults in students' lives—such as grandparents, guardians, and others—who may not be parents but are responsible for students.) Deliberately and thoughtfully involving parents and other caregivers is associated with the following:

♦ Higher grade-point averages;

♦ Increased reading achievement and mathematics;

♦ Better homework skills;

♦ Decreased dropout rates;

♦ Improved social skills; and

♦ Good self-regulating behavior.[25]

Therefore, the teacher's disposition toward parent involvement as well as the ability to involve parents is tied to students' academic success.

How Can Caregivers Become Involved at School or at Home in Their Students' Education?

Parent involvement research shows that parents are most likely to become involved with their children's education when they perceive that their involvement is desired and valued.[26] There are two primary venues for caregiver involvement: at school and at home.

School Involvement

The use of classroom volunteers is a common practice in elementary schools but it declines in the upper grades. Teachers using classroom volunteers may develop "job descriptions" to let volunteers know what is expected and needed.[27] A teacher may have a work folder available for a regular volunteer that is organized with the names of the students with whom the volunteer will be working as well as any necessary materials. The volunteer would know to pick up the folder so that valuable instruction time is not interrupted by the teacher having to find work for the volunteer. Furthermore, workshops to train volunteers about how to provide specific support in the classroom

> When used appropriately, "parent classroom volunteers are the 'unsung heroes' who extend the teacher's ability to help children more effectively."[29]

can benefit student performance. To illustrate, consider the experience of a kindergarten teacher who completed an action research study in which eighteen parents volunteered to support small-group reading in the classroom over a five-month period. Students working in the small groups with volunteers demonstrated increased word recognition compared to peers who worked only with the teacher. In addition, students indicated that they liked having parents in the classroom.[28]

Home Involvement

Effective teachers recognize that the ability of parents/caregivers to be involved in their children's schooling varies. For example, a parent working second shift may see his son get off the bus in the afternoon but come home after the child is in bed, so wanting that parent to review the child's homework is not realistic. Sometimes a caregiver may want to be involved, but it is just not logistically possible. Teachers who are adept at involving caregivers understand that expectations for involvement should be clear and feasible.[30] Effective teachers work on establishing open and trusting communication with families and share with them opportunities for involvement at home and school. Actively using family members in helping with homework is one way of involving adults. Indeed, a study of 253 middle school students' families revealed that students who re-

> Interactive homework involves homework in which the caregiver and the child work with each other to complete the assignment. Interactive homework fosters positive interdependence between the caregiver and the child. One caution with interactive homework or any other type of homework is to ensure that the student has a caregiver at home and has the resources at home to complete the homework. Otherwise, assigning the homework sets the child up for failure.[33]

ceived interactive family assignments turned in more accurate work, had higher rates of completion, and increased their grades.[31] Interactive assignments also promoted family dialogue about schoolwork. Other benefits of interactive homework included better designed homework assignments.[32]

Potential Challenges

Although there are clear rewards from parent/caregiver involvement, there also are challenges. First, different perceptions between caregivers and teachers about what constitutes help can create problems. Researchers have noted that parents often report that their involvement in education includes getting students ready for school and child safety issues, whereas teachers viewed parental involvement as the presence of the caregiver in school.[34] One researcher found that parents thought teachers did not want them involved because parents were not specifically invited to participate, whereas the teachers thought general invitations were sufficient.[35] Regardless, teachers who involve caregivers in the education of children know that caregiver involvement pays dividends but requires some upfront planning and communication. Successful teachers develop relationships with their students' families and actively encourage their involvement. By offering various opportunities for involvement, teachers enable parents/caregivers to choose what works best for them.

How Does the Way Caregiver Involvement is Solicited Affect Whether Caregivers Become Involved?

Caregivers may be explicitly or implicitly invited to participate in students' schooling. An example of an explicit invitation would be if the student asks for help on homework or the teacher asks caregivers to read with their child after school. An *implicit* way in which caregivers may get involved is if their student brings home a low test grade and they help him study or request a conference with the child's teacher.[36] However, caregivers are more likely to get involved when explicitly invited. Think of it as the difference between being asked to go to a party and just knowing that a party is happening; most people are more likely to go if they are invited.

Communication channels need to be open and used regularly. Often teachers send home information in the form of a class newsletter or a request for caregivers to sign a graded test. Although both of these formats have the potential to invite caregivers to follow up with a teacher, they seldom perceive such activities as invitations to dialogue. This type of information is really one-way communication; that is, information is conveyed, but a response from the receiver is not expected. An example of two-way communication, on the other hand, is a conversation that occurs face-to-face, through written exchanges, electronically, or verbally.

As teachers refine their efforts to encourage caregiver involvement, it is important to consider how parents/caregivers perceive the various options and how their perceptions may vary from those of teachers. Figure 2.6 summarizes the findings from a case study conducted in a junior high school in which parents and teachers were interviewed about their perspectives on invitations for involvement.[37]

Figure 2.6. Parent/Caregiver and Teacher Perspectives on Involvement

Invitation for Involvement	Parent/Caregiver Perspective	Teacher Perspective
"Open door" policy	Is not perceived by caregivers as an open invitation to come into the classroom—some parents believe that a teacher would be offended if a parent wanted to come and sit in the room.	Is used to make caregivers feel comfortable coming into the classroom and/or contacting the teacher.
Newsletter	This is how teachers often tell caregivers what is occurring in the school. A common problem with newsletters being used as an invitation is that they do not include enough information about who should come, date, time, and location. Simply announcing a special activity will occur is not the same as saying "Families are invited to attend…," which cues caregivers that their presence is welcomed and desired.	Is an invitation to become involved by supporting students at home or helping at school.
Individual contacts	This approach builds relationships between teachers and parents/caregivers and expresses appreciation. Teachers who individually ask parents for help also are more likely to follow up with a thank you, which caregivers appreciate because it shows that the teacher values them.	

How Can I Effectively and Efficiently Solicit Caregivers' Potential Involvement?

Most parents/caregivers are invested in their students. These adults can serve as valuable resources for teachers—from support of the individual student to a larger commitment of support in the classroom. As supporters of their students' learning, caregivers share information that will help the teacher get to know the student as well as alert the teacher to medical and identified educational needs. Caregivers also may be willing to volunteer on a one-time or ongoing basis.

Figure 2.7 (page 24) is a student information sheet that teachers ask caregivers to complete about their student. (A reproducible blank template can be found in Part II.) For instance, the student information sheet may be completed and given to the teacher at a Back-to-School night that occurs shortly after school starts in the fall where families and

Figure 2.7. Student Information Sheet

Student Information Sheet

To be completed by the parent/caregiver

Student Name: _____

Parent/Caregiver Name(s): _____

Preferred Telephone Number to Use ☐ Home☐ Work ☐ Cell _____

Email Address: _____

You can inquire if caregivers want to opt-in to a class email list.

☐ *Check here if you would like to receive periodic updates of class assignments.*

How do you prefer that I contact you? *Check one:* ☐ Email ☐ Telephone ☐ Written Note

Please share with me talents or skills that you have that you would be willing to share with the class. *Check the box(es) below.*

☐ Volunteer outside of class
☐ Provide baked goods
☐ Collect materials that can be reused in class such as gallon milk jugs
   (teacher will contact to get specific items)
☐ Classroom volunteer working with students
☐ Classroom volunteer creating class materials
☐ Field trip chaperone
☐ Guest speaker – *tell area of interest* _____
☐ Other – *please tell how you would like to volunteer* _____

You can adapt this section to fit the needs of a particular grade level/subject area.

Tell me what I should know about your child as his/her teacher.

This offers an open-ended opportunity for caregivers to share information that they deem relevant and important in the education of their student.

Does your student have any of the following on file with the school?
Check the box(es) ☐ Medical Alert (e.g., allergy) ☐ IEP/504 Plan

This alerts the teacher to important documentation.

(*Parents:* This portion of the form is for me to keep track of my communication with you throughout the year.)

Contact Log

Date	Purpose	Person	Mode
			☐ Email ☐ Meeting ☐ Note ☐ Telephone
	For recording individual contacts as opposed to "mass contacts" such as Back-to-School night.		☐ Email ☐ Meeting ☐ Note ☐ Telephone
			☐ Email ☐ Meeting ☐ Note ☐ Telephone
			☐ Email ☐ Meeting ☐ Note ☐ Telephone

Please return this sheet to your student's teacher.

students informally meet the teacher. Students can also take the information form to their caregivers the first day of school to be filled out.

Finally, the information sheet does not always have to be a beginning-of-the-school-year document. Teachers in schools with semester block scheduling may find the sheet appropriate when they get a new roster of students. Likewise, it is useful to have caregivers complete the information sheet for students who transfer into the class later in the year. Finally, the information sheet may be sent home midyear with a request that caregivers complete it so that the teacher has updated information. Asking for the information conveys to the parents/caregivers that their involvement will enhance the education of their child as well as that of the other students in the classroom.

Summary

Dispositions are the attitudes and beliefs that undergird teachers' decisions and actions. Although learning about and using appropriate teaching techniques and ways to assess students is certainly necessary for a teacher to be effective, the intangibles of caring about students, interacting with students on a personal level, and welcoming and engaging caregivers also support the effectiveness of teachers in the classroom. After all, most time what is remembered most about memorable teachers are those who demonstrated that they cared and who took the time to get to know their students.

Notes

1   McGavin, 2006, ¶5.

2   S. Penn (personal communication, November 15, 2009).

3   *The Best Teacher Ever*, n.d.

4   Swope, 2004, p. 18.

5   Anderson, 2005, p. 144.

6   Google search conducted on September 1, 2008.

7   Allen, Witt, & Wheeless, 2006.

8   Allday & Pakurar, 2007.

9   Robinson, 2007.

10 Pogue & AhYun, 2006.

11 Robinson, 2007, p. 22.

12 Taylor & Wasicsko, 2000, p. 9.

13 *The Way We See It*, 2004.

14 Peart & Campbell, 1999.

15 Cassidy & Bates, 2005, pp. 94–95.

16 Ilmer, Snyder, Erbaugh, & Kurtz, 1997; Zeichner, 2003.

17 Baker, 1999; Bernard, 2003; Corbett & Wilson, 2004; Pressley, Raphael, Gallagher, & DiBella, 2004.

18 Ferguson, 2002.

19 Peart & Campbell, 1999.

20 Peart & Campbell, 1999; Wentzel, 1997; Younger & Warrington, 1999.

21 Collinson, Killeavy, & Stephenson, 1999; Peart & Campbell, 1999.

22 Agne, 1992; Collinson, et al., 1999; Csikszentmihalyi, et al., 1993; Ford & Trotman, 2001; Younger & Warrington, 1999.

23 Gannon, 2004.

24 Baum & McMurray, 2004.

25 Anderson & Minke, 2007; Baum & McMurray-Schwarz, 2004; Deslandes & Bertrand, 2005.

26 See for example, Anderson & Minke, 2007; Deslandes & Bertrand, 2005; Halsey, 2005.

27 Carlisle, Stanley, & Kemple, 2005.

28 DeCusati & Johnson, 2004.

29 DeCusati & Johnson, 2004, p. 243.

30 Carlisle, et al., 2005.

31 Van Voorhis, 2003.

32 Van Voorhis, 2003.

33 Grant, Stronge, & Popp, 2008.

34 Anderson & Minke, 2007.

35 Halsey, 2005.

36 Deslandes & Bertrand, 2005.

37 Halsey, 2005.

3

What Knowledge Do Teachers Need to Support Teaching and Learning?

Walking into a classroom as the teacher-of-record for the first time is nearly overwhelming. Every teacher has classroom experience as a student, but *being* the teacher is decidedly different from how he or she spent seventeen years in the classroom on the other side of the desk or, for that matter, in four years of undergraduate teacher preparation. Standing before a sea of faces, all of the new teacher's accumulated knowledge and preparation need to come together. There are many kinds of knowledge—explicit, implicit, tacit, innate, and learned—but in the final analysis, the label does not matter so much, except perhaps as an indication of where the knowledge originated.

Teachers come to the classroom with varying amounts of education, experience, and preparation. Teachers also choose to hone their knowledge and skills through professional development and some even share their knowledge with others new to the field or with those struggling in the profession. Regardless, at any stage of development, a teacher possesses a level of knowledge that makes him or her more or less effective in the classroom. So, then, the question remains: What knowledge do teachers need to support teaching and learning? Although there are many answers to this question, this chapter focuses on the following:

- ◆ Knowledge through subject matter preparation, certification, and experience
- ◆ Knowledge of how to communicate effectively
- ◆ Knowledge gained through professional development
- ◆ Knowledge passed down through mentoring others

Knowledge Through Subject-Matter Preparation, Certification, and Experience

How Much Does Subject-Matter Knowledge Matter?

First, let's acknowledge that subject-matter knowledge matters. Educators and students alike recognize the importance of a firm grounding in the content. When educators, including teachers and administrators, have been asked to identify what makes an effective teacher, they offer subject-matter knowledge as a major criterion.[1] Students also recognize the importance of teachers knowing their subject areas. Whether a teacher is working with at-risk students or students of high ability, students respect a teacher who knows his or her "stuff."[2] Consider the research studies cited in Figure 3.1 related to the impact of content area expertise.

Figure 3.1. Subject-Matter Knowledge and Teacher Effectiveness

Related Findings	Citation
◆ When math teachers majored in mathematics, their students perform better.	Floden & Meniketti, 2005
◆ One research study of the relationship between the number of courses completed and student achievement found that there was little increased benefit for student achievement when a teacher had taken more than five mathematics courses, indicating that the students actually benefited more when their teachers took coursework in how to teach mathematics rather than completing more content courses.	Monk, 1994
◆ A study of high school teachers in North Carolina examined the effects of teacher performance on subject matter as well as of general pedagogy tests on student achievement. The researchers found that a one standard deviation difference in teachers' scores in mathematics was associated with a 0.03 standard deviation difference in student achievement in mathematics.	Clotfelter, Ladd, & Vigdor, 2007
◆ Certification in the subject area that a teacher teaches has a positive effect on student achievement. Certification in mathematics increases student achievement by 0.12 standard deviation. Similar results are found in high school English. Student achievement in English I classrooms taught by teachers without certification in English was negatively affected.	Clotfelter, Ladd, & Vigdor, 2007

The effects of subject matter knowledge, or a lack thereof, can be found in other areas that have indirect effects on student learning. Specifically, subject matter knowledge is associated with the following:

- Effectiveness in teaching gifted students. One challenge for teachers without extensive content knowledge is teaching gifted children, who often need to be challenged with in-depth subject-matter knowledge. Lack of subject-matter knowledge impacts teaching, as teachers cannot accelerate learners through the curriculum or effectively remediate learners when they do not have an understanding of the intricacies of the content.[3]

- More confidence when teaching.[4]

- Increased enthusiasm about what the teachers are teaching.[5]

Regardless, teachers feel more confident and can teach concepts with more accuracy and more depth when they know the subject matter they are teaching. Indeed, one researcher wrote, "it appears that teachers' subject-matter knowledge is related to their teaching approaches (pedagogy)."[6]

How Much Does Certification Matter?

Teaching situations differ with regards to the requirement for certification. A reality in public education in the United States is that applicants need to be licensed in the area in which they teach and administrators need to make sure that the applicant either possesses the necessary certification or is awaiting certification and that teachers are certified. Figure 3.2 (page 32) provides a sample of selected research related to certification and student achievement as well as other effects.

In summary, certification does, indeed, matter when it comes to student achievement, and it makes for a more confident teacher in the classroom. Certification supports the teaching and learning process by ensuring that teachers have knowledge in both the subject matter they teach and how to teach the subject matter, as well as the evidence that teachers have met licensing requirements developed by each individual state.

Figure 3.2. Certification and Student Achievement as Well as Other Effects

Related Findings	Citation
♦ Certified teachers assigned to teach in their area of certification are more effective than those teaching out-of-field or who are not certified.	Darling-Hammond, 2000; Darling-Hammond, Berry, & Thoreson, 2001; Goldhaber & Brewer, 2000; Hawk, Coble, & Swanson, 1985
♦ Teachers report a decrease in efficacy when assigned to teach a subject outside their field.	Ross, Cousins, Gadalla, & Hannay, 1999
♦ Students of uncertified teachers had grade-equivalent scores two months behind their peers who were taught by certified teachers.	Laczko-Kerr & Berliner, 2002
♦ In a study of high school teachers in North Carolina that examined the effects of certification on student achievement, the researchers found that teachers with temporary or provisional licenses have a negative effect on student achievement.	Clotfelter, Ladd, & Vigdor, 2007
♦ Teachers who have educational coursework are knowledgeable about how students learn and how to package material for student learning, resulting in a link between pedagogy and student performance.	Ferguson & Womack, 1993

How Much Does Experience Matter?

A substantial body of research exists regarding the relationship between teaching experience and student achievement. We intuitively know that often the longer one does something, the better one gets. (There are, of course, caveats to this, such as how good one is to begin with and whether one continues to improve.) For example, a child who has a propensity toward artistic expression attempts a first drawing. The first drawing is certainly not as good as the tenth, twenty-fifth, or one-hundredth. The same is true for teaching. Figure 3.3 provides a sample of research related to teaching experience and student achievement.

Figure 3.3. Teaching Experience and Student Achievement

Related Findings	Citation
♦ Teachers experience seemingly exponential growth the first few years they are in the profession, but the growth curve levels off (around years five to eight).	Darling-Hammond, 2000; Sanders, 2001
♦ Students of teachers with more experience often have higher levels of achievement than peers taught by less-experienced teachers.	Fetler, 1999; Glass, 2002; Wenglinsky, 2000
♦ Novice teachers (one to two years' experience) were less effective than teachers with some experience.	Clotfelter, Ladd, & Vigdor, 2007
♦ Teachers who stay in the teaching profession become more effective and the effects peak at years twenty-one to twenty-seven.	Clotfelter, Ladd, & Vigdor, 2007

Indeed, the differences between how novice and veteran teachers go about planning, teaching, and managing the classroom vary greatly. Figure 3.4 shows the differences between those with less experience and those who have been in the classroom and honed their knowledge and skills.

Figure 3.4. Differences between Novice and More Experienced Teachers

Novice teachers...	*More experienced* teachers...
♦ Focus on keeping order[7] ♦ Focus on learning the curriculum in order to teach it—often literally[8] ♦ Move toward solutions quickly without developing an understanding of the issue to inform their actions[9]	♦ Have well-developed routines that minimize disruptions to learning[10] ♦ Are more reflective in their practice[11] ♦ View planning in terms of both long-term and short-term needs[12]

Although novice teachers are at the left of the developmental continuum, they learn on the job how to manage the many responsibilities of teaching and learning, and how to do so in a seamless fashion. As novice teachers become more experienced teachers, they develop the skills necessary to positively effect student achievement. Experience is the best teacher and this rings particularly true in education. Teachers gain foundational knowledge in teacher-preparation programs and then continue to build their knowledge through experience in the classroom.

A new-to-the-profession first-year teacher is called a novice, but at what point in a career is a teacher no longer a "novice" and considered an "experienced" teacher? For many teachers, the transition from novice to experienced teacher is evident sometime during the third year of teaching. Competence and duly earned confidence is evident. True, a few teachers transition earlier and others later. As teachers continue to develop, they shift from mastering the elements of the job to dissecting, analyzing, and enhancing their professional practices. In essence, they become "experts" of teaching and serve as mentors, teacher leaders, and perform other services to the profession. Research has found that experienced expert teachers do the following:

- Provide targeted observations about what occurs in the classroom.[13]

- Monitor, understand, and interpret events with insightful detail.[14]

- Design lessons that motivate students.[15]

- Analyze learning from students' perspective.[16]

- Use mental planning to anticipate the flow of a lesson in order to adjust before teaching the lesson to students.[17]

- Consider theory as it relates to the content and then create a concrete experience for classroom implementation.[18]

- Rely on routines to streamline the planning process.[19]

- Include adaptations for specific learners within the lesson and respond to students' performance.[20]

- Can explain where a lesson fits within a larger context.[21]

Knowledge of How to Communicate

Why Does Communication Matter?

It is communication—between teachers and students, teachers and teachers, as well as students and students—that allows learning to take place. Despite the saying that "talk is cheap," there is inherent value in communication. In fact, researchers have studied pedagogic discourse (i.e., teacher talk) over the past several years.[22] Teacher talk is how many educators communicate the business of school and the knowledge and skills of a content area to their students. Teachers' ability to communicate with their students influences student performance as teachers are providing students with the knowledge, skills, and abilities necessary to learn and use new material.[23] For example, a preservice teacher assigned to tape record a lesson she taught and analyze the discourse reflected that her initial impression while she was teaching that students were learning the material was inaccurate, as by listening to the dialogue she identified areas of concern in what students were saying and she identified where she needed to be more explicit about her expectations.[24] Communication skills relate to the words teachers choose, the tone and nonverbal signals they send, as well as their ability to help others comprehend their message. Despite the impact of rhetoric, many teachers have never taken a class on how to maximize their verbal ability.

What Does the Research Say About the Relationship Between a Teacher's Verbal Ability and Teacher Effectiveness?

Research related to communication skills and effective teaching reveals that a teacher's verbal ability is an indication of teacher effectiveness. Studies on verbal ability and teacher effectiveness that used standardized scores from tests such as the National Teacher Examination (later Praxis), the Graduate Record Exam, and others, have typically found a relationship between high verbal test scores and high levels of student achievement.[25] For example, students with teachers who had higher verbal abilities tended to score higher on standardized tests.[26] Yet teaching is about so much more than test scores, so let's put this in perspective. Teachers' ability to effectively communicate "influences the relationships they establish with others, the clarity of the explanations to students, and invariably, student understanding and achievement."[27] The following sections examine how communication in the classroom can be improved through a focus on two facets of verbal ability: (1) giving directions and (2) communication snafus that result in an unintended message being transmitted.

How Can Communication in the Classroom Be Improved?

By Phrasing Commands and Directions Better

How many times a day are students asked to take out a book, log onto a computer, write their names on their papers, line up, and a range of other directions? Teachers should not be dictators shouting directions, but commands are nonetheless a necessary part of teaching. Specific instructions are needed to create a smoothly functioning classroom and to prevent disruptions in instruction. Commands are classified as either alpha or beta commands, and researchers have found that students are more likely to follow alpha commands.[28] Figure 3.5 provides more detail regarding these types of commands.

Figure 3.5. Alpha and Beta Commands

Type of Command	Description	Example Command
Alpha	Succinct, direct, specific, and clear instructions	"Turn to page 115 in your math book."
Beta	Multiple and/or vague instructions	"Students, look at the time. It is time for math. Please get ready by getting out your math book and turning to page 115."

The alpha command only has one verb whereas the beta command has multiple verbs and multiple ideas communicated to the student. "Turning to page 115" may get lost when a student hears the longer command. Regardless of how the command is phrased, adequate time to respond to the command must be given. Obviously, more time is required for students to "head their papers" with their names, subject, and date than to "double-click the word-processing icon."

Changing how one delivers directions is a no-cost intervention that can pay big dividends. A small study in which teachers were trained to use effective commands, including alpha command characteristics and adequate response time, showed increased levels of compliance with directions, improvements in academic behaviors, and a decrease in misbehavior.[29] Providing well-phrased commands and instructions enhances classroom management as students know what is expected of them. When students know and understand what to do, they are more likely to do it, which increases student engagement and, in turn, student achievement.[30]

By Avoiding Potential Pitfalls in Communication

Teachers are in a position of authority, and both the best and the worst in our profession are responsible for the social, physical, and academic well-being and growth of students in their classrooms. "The messages teachers convey to their students through the use of language can often go unconsidered, yet such practices can have a significant impact on students and their schooling."[31] For example, consider what was observed as part of a study on teacher-student discourse:[32]

> A primary-level student brought a horse bridle for "show and tell" that his father had given him. His first and only uninterrupted sentence indicated that he was excited. The teacher corrected the student's incorrect pronoun use and began questioning the student about the buckle, which related to a prior week's spelling word. Every time the student spoke, even just one word, the teacher corrected his language use. At the end of the exchange, the teacher called the student a "good boy." The teacher's zeal to correct language resulted in a student not being able to share what he had been excited to bring and being denied an opportunity to speak on a subject about which he was knowledgeable. In the end, the teacher's only praise of the student was when he said "yes" instead of "yeah" in compliance with her interruptions.

Did the teacher intend to curtail the student? She probably did not mean to, yet that was the effect. Much more damaging is that the teacher's actions undermined the student's confidence in his speaking ability and willingness to speak publicly.[33] Figure 3.6 provides another example of how communication mistakes can have unintended consequences.

**Figure 3.6. Students Interrupting Each Other—
What Does This Communicate?**

Situation *Note:* This is one example from a five-month study involving twenty-four hours of recorded discourse	Student A was asked by the teacher to answer a question, while Student B desperately tried to interrupt to provide a response. When Student A did not provide the expected answer, Student B verbally "jumped in" and gave the correct answer. The teacher turned her attention from the student she had originally called upon (Student A) to the interloper (Student B) and began a dialogue with Student B about why the response was correct, in the process forgetting all about Student A.
What just happened?	The teacher's actions communicated different behavioral expectations for the student who interrupted because he was allowed to correct Student A. That is, the teacher accorded Student B a higher social position by failing to reprimand him for breaking classroom rules not to interrupt when somebody has been called upon to respond and by rephrasing his explanation for the benefit of the class. At the conclusion of the yearlong observation period, the researcher noted that at the beginning of the year Student B rarely contributed in a productive manner in class, but by the end of the year he became more willing to participate productively, three times the rate of the class average. This increase in participation by Student B is a dual-edged sword as it comes at a cost to the other students.
Why did this happen?	The teacher indicated in followup discussions with the researcher that the pressure of insufficient time had a lot to do with her push to move forward on a lesson. Thus, it is important to remember that providing individual "well-structured, engaged, and responsive verbal support" (p. 358) requires time.
How can this be countered?	The researcher recommended using small-group work and ensuring that all students have opportunities to participate and that expectations for all students are equitable.

Source: Table based on an article by Black, 2004.

How Can Teachers Reflect Upon Their Communication?

Everyone has done it, whether professionally or personally. We have all been in situations where we have scratched our heads wondering how in the world we got ourselves in a predicament when all we said was, " _____ " (fill in the blank). Sometimes what we say and what is heard are two very different messages. In the rapid pace of a classroom, often there is not enough time to carefully compose, filter, review, and revise one's thoughts before speaking. So it is important for teachers to word the message as carefully as possible the first time, whether in terms of how directions are given or how content is explained (see scenario presented in sidebar).

A parent contacts her son's teacher to say that her child was uncomfortable because the teacher called on boys and corrected boys' behavior more than girls. The teacher is surprised and conveys that she enjoys having the child in her class. The parent then reasserts that she thought the teacher should know of her son's concerns. Upon reflection the teacher realized that the student's perception was accurate, but not for the reason the parent and child were concerned; rather, the class demographics were 17 boys and 8 girls. So the teacher followed up with the parent by sending a note in which she shared the demographics and encouraged the parent or student to let her know of any other concerns.

Teacher talk can be observed. In fact, using an outside observer often yields more insights than using a videotape or audio recording of yourself, because the other person can not only make notes of what was said but may also remember the context and the tone used to deliver the message. An observer also can provide feedback as a teacher reflects on his or her teacher talk. Consider the following situation:

A mentor teacher observed Ms. Johnson leading a lesson early in the school year that involved note taking. Some low murmuring was occurring in the classroom at the time of the observation as the teacher had instructed students to ask a neighbor if they had missed something. Then the teacher asked for quiet, and the students' demonstrated disrespect by dropping their pencils on the floor. Ms. Johnson did not do any immediate followup with her students, despite the lack of respect shown for her. After class, the mentor teacher and Ms. Johnson talked about respectful interactions with students and classroom management using the *Communication Observation Record* (see Figure 3.7) as a means to reflect upon incident.

Figure 3.7. Communication Observation Record

Teacher Said	Response	Meant
I want it so quiet that I can hear a pin drop. (used a louder voice than the one she was using to give notes—sounded agitated—this was the first request for quiet)	☒ **Complied** ☐ **Did not respond** ☒ **Adversarial verbal/ nonverbal language** Most of the students held their pens out and dropped them on the floor.	I wanted the students quiet so that they could hear the next important point I was going to make. **Follow up to be done:** ☒ **No** ☐ **Yes** (*specify*)

The *Communication Observation Record* in Figure 3.7 offers a way for teachers to consider their communication with others and to reflect on the possible effects of their messages. Essentially, this reflection involves three steps.

1. Remember as accurately as possible what you said.

2. Picture the person who gave you the response. What was the response? How did the person look when he or she gave the response? What was the facial expression or body language? How would you characterize the response overall: compliant, ignoring, adversarial, or something else?

3. What did you intend for the person to hear?

The steps followed when observing teacher talk with the *Communication Observation Record* are essentially the same as those used when mentally reflecting. The difference is that an observer can write down verbatim what was said and facilitate the discussion of how teacher talk was used in the classroom or other situation, such as meetings.

In the first column of Figure 3.7, the observer records word-for-word what the teacher said. In the second column, the observer indicates the general nature of the response and includes a brief clarifying note. The last, shaded, column is completed after the lesson/meeting is over. This is where interpretation and explanations are recorded. When using this format, it is suggested that the observer read to the teacher what he or she said and then ask:

1. Was the response of the person what you expected?

2. What did you intend for the person to hear?

After discussing the teacher talk, the observer can indicate in the final column if the teacher plans to follow up with the person and what the followup will entail. Depending on the situation, it may be helpful to the teacher to role play the followup with the observer. Also, the observer can check with the teacher later to see how the followup went. In the case of our fictional teacher, Ms. Johnson, she and her mentor discussed why it is frustrating for students to have the teacher communicate one direction (i.e., talk with a neighbor), and then scold the students for following that direction. So they discussed ways for the teacher earn back some respect and authority that would concurrently result in better classroom management.

Knowledge Gained Through Professional Development

Some people go to college planning to enter the education profession, whereas others are pulled toward education later in life because of love for a particular content area. For teachers employed in public school settings, likely the first knowledge they actively sought to enter the education profession was related to teacher certification. Once employed, they acquired more knowledge through experience, and they also gained knowledge via professional development and reflection.

What Does the Research Say About the Positive Impact of Professional Development and Student Learning?

The reality is that teachers are the single most influential school-related factor in student learning.[34] Teachers, like students, are very different on their first day in the classroom versus when they exit the classroom on the last day of their teaching career. Ideally, they have

> "Teachers can and do make a difference and consistently high quality teaching, supported by strategic professional development, can and does deliver dramatic improvements in student learning."[35]

grown, improved, shared, innovated, and reflected. Figure 3.8 provides a sample of research regarding the professional development.

Figure 3.8. Findings Relating Professional Development and Teacher Effectiveness

Major Findings	Study
Teachers who participate in professional development related to their content area have students with higher achievement scores than colleagues who did not participate in professional development.	Camphire, 2001; Cross & Regden, 2002; Wenglinsky, 2002
Professional development has a positive impact on teachers' attitudes and perceptions of preparedness to implement standards-based teaching.	Heck, Banilower, Weiss, & Rosenberg, 2008
A meta-analysis of more than 500,000 studies reported the following effect sizes: feedback to students (1.13), direct instruction (0.82), classroom environment (0.56), mastery learning (0.5), and questioning (0.41). The meta-analysis suggests that professional development on these topics would have a positive impact. *Note:* The numbers in parentheses are the effect sizes, which are a measurement of how much impact a particular item has when comparing different groups; the numbers range from a low of 0 for no impact to a high of 2.	Hattie, 2003
Middle school math teachers who received training in (1) content standards, (2) curriculum materials, (3) effective calculator usage, or (4) instructional methods had higher average student test scores than their colleagues who did not receive training. Interestingly, the same study found that teachers who reported receiving small or moderate amounts of professional development had students who outperformed teacher who said they had a large amount. *Note:* The terms (i.e., small, moderate, large) were not defined in the study.	Telese, 2008
Teachers who received three days of professional development in reading strategies, tools, and techniques were effective in reducing the number of kindergartners identified as being at-risk for reading difficulties.	Scanlon, Gelzheiser, Vellutino, Schatschneider, & Sweeney, 2008
A researcher found that professional development had some influenced teachers' practices, which, in turn, linked to student achievement. An interesting finding from the analysis was that most of the difference between teachers in their practices is not accounted for by professional development. The researcher suggests that factors unique to the teacher (e.g., individual style) are likely responsible and warrant study.	Wallace, 2009

What Constitutes Effective Professional Development for Teachers?

Worthwhile professional development pursuits are relevant, timely, interactive, and offer tools and insights that teachers can use. They "engage the hearts and heads of educators in order to keep teachers engaged in active learning."[36] Effective teachers know their students and realize that participating in professional growth activities that lead to a deeper understanding of students' cultural backgrounds can be beneficial.[37] Effective professional development opportunities share a common theme in that they build the individual teacher capacity so that high standards are nurtured.

One-size-fits-all professional development rarely meets the needs of all teachers. Sadly, teachers perceive that they do not have much input on the topics or delivery method of professional development. When teachers do have such input they are more likely to actively participate.[38]

The checklist[39] below highlights some critical attributes to aid in professional development planning efforts throughout the year. It provides guidance about critical components that can change teaching practices.

The professional development I am planning:

☐ Is based on the needs of teachers in my building or school district.

☐ Connects student performance standards with teachers' work.

☐ Immerses teachers in experimentation.

☐ Provides intensive and sustained support for teachers.

☐ Links directly to how teachers work in the classroom.

☐ Involves the teachers in concrete training.

☐ Increases teachers' content skills by focusing on subject matter.

☐ Includes structures for collaboration with other teachers.

☐ Connects with the overall vision and mission of the school and school district.

☐ Will be supported by the administrator implementing the professional development.

Many teachers find themselves at some point in their teaching careers teaching a subject that they are not comfortable teaching because of inadequate preparation and knowledge. Take George Graphy, for example. George has been teaching world geography at the middle school level for 10 years. His district revamped the social studies curriculum and decided to infuse geography into the other social studies areas rather than offering it as a separate course. George must begin teaching ancient civilizations next fall. George has a social science endorsement but most of his undergraduate coursework is in geography. To gain confidence and fill in some knowledge gaps, a little professional development in the subject area is just what George needs.

The *Professional Development Plan* in Figure 3.9 (page 42) offers a way that George, or any teacher, can plan his professional development. (A blank reproducible template of the *Professional Development Plan* is available in Part II.) The teacher begins by setting a goal,

Figure 3.9. Sample Completed Professional Development Plan

Professional's Name:	Subject/Grade Level:
George Graphy	*Middle School Social Sciences*

Goal(s):
To obtain content knowledge about ancient civilizations.

Possible Steps/Strategies:	Time Frame:	Cost:
☑ University/College Course Options:		
HIST 482—Survey of Ancient Civilizations	July—August, 2 nights per week	$652
HIST 463—Incan and Mayan Civilizations	July—August, 2 nights per week	$652
☑ Self-Study Options:		
Read *A History of the Ancient World* by Chester G. Starr	July—August	$62.00
Visit Smithsonian Museum of Natural History	July—one weekend	$350 travel costs
☑ Summer Training Options:		
Teacher Summer Institute—King Tut: Unwrapped	July—one week	$600
Ancient African Civilizations	July—two-week residency	No cost; $400 stipend

Final Decision:
Attend the Summer Teacher Institute and read *A History of the Ancient World*.

thus identifying the area of need. Then, possible steps or strategies to achieve the goal are specified. The following are the three main options for professional development:

♦ *University/College Courses*—Local colleges and universities are great resources for taking courses related to a specific content area. Some may offer courses specifically designed for teachers.

♦ *Self-Study*—Teachers can engage in self-study by reading books, participating in online book discussions, watching DVDs on the subject area, or by visiting museums during summer vacations.

♦ *Summer Training Options*—Summer training options may be available from many different sources. For example, local school districts may offer summer workshops on teaching specific content. Local museums and organizations may hold summer institutes. The key is to explore all the opportunities available.

For each option, George considers the time and cost involved (see Figure 3.9). These are often determining factors in which option to pursue. Finally, based on myriad factors, the teacher makes the decision on how best to meet the goal, and he or she starts pursuing it.

Ultimately, George decides to pursue two options: (1) read *A History of the Ancient World* by Chester G. Starr and (2) attend a Teacher Summer Institute called "King Tut: Unwrapped" offered by a local museum. George would have liked to attend the summer residency on "Ancient African Civilizations," but he cannot be away from home for the two-week program. His school district is willing to pay for the Teacher Summer Institute offered by the museum as long as George agrees to provide professional development to other teachers. Finally, George decides to read the book because he will gain information about ancient civilizations other than Egypt.

Sharing Professional Knowledge with Others Through Mentoring[a]

Teacher mentoring is "an intentional pairing of an inexperienced person with an experienced partner to guide and nurture his or her development."[40] Although formal teacher mentoring programs have become more common, mentoring itself is not a particularly new idea. Indeed, our contemporary use of the word *mentor* harkens back to Greek mythology, when Odysseus placed his son in the care of Mentor—a wise, experienced, and trusted friend. These same three adjectives describe our current concept of a mentor as well. That is, a veteran teacher who serves as a mentor to a new teacher should be *wise, experienced,* and *trusted*. Our understanding of (1) the *goals* of teacher mentoring, (2) the *roles* that mentors should fulfill, and (3) the *effects* of mentoring on teacher retention/development has deepened considerably in recent years.

Why Does Teacher Mentoring Matter?

School districts must do more than attract and hire qualified teachers; they also must *retain* them. What's more, districts must help their teachers *develop* as professionals.[41] In an effort to address the dual aims of retaining qualified teachers and developing beginning teachers into effective professionals, many districts have turned to *teacher mentoring*.

Mentoring in the teaching field aims to retain qualified teachers and to help new teachers develop into highly effective professionals. To achieve these aims, mentoring may be characterized as pursuing three broad goals:[42]

♦ *Vocational support*—Support that focuses on the essential practices and responsibilities of classroom teachers, such as knowledge of curriculum, the

___

a The mentoring section was contributed by Dr. Christopher Gareis, a colleague at The College of William and Mary.

use of differentiated instructional strategies, and establishing effective routines in the classroom.[43]

♦ *Psychosocial support*—New teachers are confronted with a plethora of challenges during their first year in the classroom, including the adjustment to overwhelming workloads and the realization that the experience of full-time teaching may not be what they expected.[44] For these reasons, novice teachers are apt to feel a lack of sufficient professional and emotional support.[45]

♦ *Role modeling*—Guide novice teachers in emulating the constructive, effective, and professional practices of experienced colleagues.[46]

What Does the Research Say are the Effects of Teacher Mentoring?

Studies conducted by researchers such as Linda Darling-Hammond and William Sanders document the influence of years of teaching experience on teacher effectiveness.[47] As stated in the section on teaching experience earlier in the chapter, studies show that teachers with one to two years experience are less effective than teachers with three or more years.[48] However, in the absence of years of experience, a constructive mentoring experience for beginning teachers can go far in helping novices perform more like veteran teachers.[49]

What Roles Can Mentors Fulfill in Support of Novice Teachers?

Mentoring makes a difference. Research tells us that mentoring programs can increase the retention level of new teachers and promote teacher effectiveness.[50] *Retaining new teachers* and *developing them as professionals* are aims of effective teacher mentoring, and they are central to our ultimate mission of improving student learning.

Mentor teachers can provide support to novice teachers simply through the example of their own professional practices. However, experience, alone, is not enough to make a veteran teacher an effective mentor. *Clarification of* and even *training in* the essential roles of mentors are often vital to a successful mentoring program.[51]

Mentor teachers can fulfill four interrelated roles to support novice teachers both personally and professionally. The accompanying figure visually depicts the fundamental roles of mentor teachers. Adapted from a synthesis of the work of several noted scholars in the field of teacher mentoring, this framework may be used by a district to assist in planning mentor training.[52]

Relating

As suggested in Figure 3.10, the foundation of effective mentoring is the fostering, nurturing, and maintaining of a *trusting relationship*. Therefore, mentoring begins with—and also continuously builds—a professional and personal relationship between the mentor and the new teacher.

Figure 3.10. Fundamental Roles of a Mentor Teacher

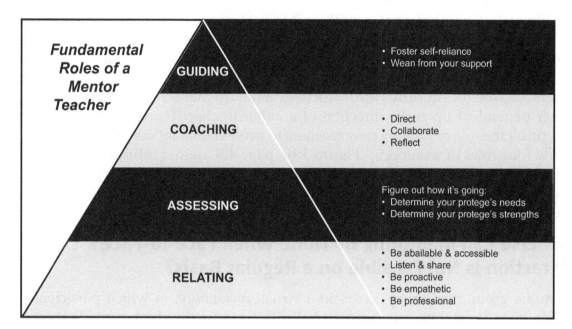

Assessing

The mentor also fulfills the role of identifying the particular strengths the new teacher exhibits, as well as the challenges the novice may be facing. The assessing role of a mentor is to *figure out how it's going,* as opposed to being evaluative or judgmental. This is an essential feature of mentor training, and veteran teachers may be equipped with a variety of strategies for assessing new teachers' needs, such as peer observation techniques, teacher and student work sample review methodology, and interactive journaling.[53]

Coaching

Once struggles and strengths have been identified, the mentor can fulfill the central role of *coaching*, which is most effective when the mentor is able to proficiently move among three complementary coaching approaches, depending upon the needs, abilities, and demeanor of the new teacher. These three coaching approaches may be characterized as:

♦ *Directive*—Mentor teachers offer explicit advice, resources, or explanations to new teachers.

♦ *Collaborative*—Mentors engage in mutual problem solving with protégés.

♦ *Reflective*—Mentors support their protégés by serving as sounding boards; they are trusted colleagues with whom to share and discuss ideas, impressions, or plans.

Guiding

Ultimately, the role of mentor teachers is to *guide* new teachers to become self-reliant, autonomous teachers who can stand on their own two professional feet. Although mentoring is an ongoing relationship, at some point protégés must move out of that identity. All teachers must be capable of expertly exercising their professional duties every day in their classrooms. An early career teacher cannot do that if his or her performance is forever dependent upon the direction of another teacher. Therefore, mentor teachers must fulfill the role of guiding new teachers to professional independence.

The four roles of mentoring (Figure 3.10, page 45) are not intuitively known to all veteran teachers, which is why mentor training is essential to the success of a mentoring program. Indeed, an investment in mentor training is worth the necessary time and expense.

How Else Can Mentoring Be Done When Face-to-Face Interaction Is Not Feasible on a Regular Basis?

Online group mentoring occurs in a *virtual community*, in which participants exchange ideas, share their experiences, challenge their assumptions, provide encouragement, offer insights, identify effective practices, construct new understandings, and prompt action. Harnessing the potential power of such a professional learning community for the use and benefit of new teachers is a compelling idea. However, just as with a more traditional community of practice, such as an instructional team, a study group, a department, or a school's faculty, a virtual community must be carefully planned to ensure that it is:

♦ *Intentional*—serves the purpose of the organization.

♦ *Constructive*—adds genuine value to the professional practice of teachers.

♦ *Feasible*—can be efficiently and effectively used within teachers' professional lives.

The reproducible resource *Planning for Online Group Mentoring* (available in Part II) offers a series of questions that may be used by school or district personnel in designing, constructing, and launching an online group mentoring forum.

Summary

Professional knowledge—whether gained through teaching experience, professional development experiences, or working with a mentor—contributes to the increased effectiveness of teachers. Teachers gain professional knowledge by reading books, attending professional conferences, and trying new instructional strategies in the classroom. The sum of these experiences serves not only to increase knowledge but also to improve skills in teaching. New knowledge and improved skill can in turn affect a teacher's disposition toward his or her work. Although this book separates dispositions (Chapter 2), knowledge (Chapter 3), and skills (Chapter 4), these three elements merge together to form an effective teacher.

Notes

1 Covino & Iwanicki, 1996; Peart & Campbell, 1999.

2 Maddux, Samples-Lachman, & Cummings, 1985; Singham, 2003.

3 VanTassel-Baska & Stambaugh, 2005.

4 Kinach, 2002.

5 Pavlou, 2004.

6 Pavlou, 2004, p. 43.

7 EGMTL Center Curriculum: Teacher Planning and Decision Making, n.d.

8 Westerman, 1991.

9 Borko & Livingston, 1989.

10 Covino & Iwanicki, 1996.

11 Covino & Iwanicki, 1996; Fetler, 1999; Reynolds, 1992.

12 Covino & Iwanicki, 1996; Fetler, 1999; Reynolds, 1992.

13 Cushing, Sabers, & Berliner, 1992.

14 Sabers, Cushing, & Berliner, 1991.

15 Karsenti & Thibert, 1998.

16 Westerman, 1991.

17 Westerman, 1991.

18 Panasuk & Sullivan, 1998.

19 Leinhart & Greeno, 1986.

20 EGMTL Center Curriculum: Teacher Planning and Decision Making, n.d.; Fuchs, Fuchs, & Phillips, 1994.

21 Allington, 2002.

22 Gale & Cosgrove, 2004, p. 125.

23 Stronge, Tucker, & Hindman, 2003; Thwaite & Rivalland, 2009.

24 Thwaite & Rivalland, 2009.

25 Ehrenberg & Brewer, 1995; Gitomer, Latham, & Ziomek, 1999; Rowan, Chiang, & Miller, 1997.

26 Strauss & Sawyer, 1986.

27 Stronge, Tucker, & Hindman, 2004, p. 9.

28 Williams & Forehand, 1984.

29 Matheson & Shriver, 2005.

30 Good & Brophy, 1997; Matheson & Shriver, 2005; Wang, Haertel, & Walberg, 1993.

31 Gale & Cosgrove, 2004, p. 125.

32 Gale & Cosgrove, 2004.

33 Gale & Cosgrove, 2004.

34 Stronge, 2007.

35 Rowe, 2004, p. 18.

36 Peery, 2004, p. 15.

37 Sleeter, 2001; Wenglinsky, 2000.

38 Coalition for Psychology in Schools and Education, 2006.

39 Compiled from resources synthesized from Adams, 2000; Supovitz, 2000.

40 Pitton, 2006, p. 1.

41 Stronge, Gareis, & Little, 2006.

42 Ensher, Heum, & Blanchard, 2003.

43 Wilson, Ireton, & Wood, 1997.

44 Abbott, 2003; Ralph, 1998.

45 Chubbock, Clift, Allard, & Quinlan, 2001; Hammerness, 2003.

46 Ensher et al., 2003.

47 Darling-Hammond, 2000; Sanders, 2001.

48 Clotfelter, Ladd, & Vigdor, 2007.

49 Fletcher & Barrett, 2004.

50 Alvarado, 2006; Darling-Hammond, 1997; Smith, & Ingersoll, 2004.

51 Gareis, 2005; Nielson, Barry, & Addison, 2006.

52 Pitton, 2006; Portner, 2003; Rudney & Guillaume, 2003.

53 Gareis, 2005.

4

What Teacher Skills Are Necessary for a Positive Learning Environment?

Effective teachers and instructional leaders have long known that "the first line of defense in managing student behavior is effective instruction."[1] There are some teachers who manage their classrooms largely through compelling instruction, and underneath the instruction there is an expectation for student ownership in the learning process. When students have defined responsibilities in the classroom they learn how to be contributing members in both their learning environment and in society; without students' involvement in self-regulating their behaviors, even the best planned lesson is likely to fail.[2] And, if lesson plans fail consistently, then student achievement is affected.

So what teacher skills are necessary for a positive learning environment? In this chapter, we explore the following teacher skills:

- Developing learning environment basics (i.e., classroom organization, cultural responsiveness, rules, and routines).

- Encouraging student ownership in the classroom.

- Effectively using time in and out of the classroom.

Learning Environment Basics

Why Does the Learning Environment Matter?

The learning environment matters because of the benefits of a productive, positive classroom. These include:[3]

- Increased student engagement.

- Decreased disruptive behavior.

- Better use of instructional time.

- Improved student achievement.

Classroom management and organization are like living a healthy lifestyle. Some teachers have developed and honed practices and routines so that instructional time is optimized and students and teachers fluidly work together. Effective teachers provide students appropriate and timely support in maintaining a productive learning environment, much like some people eat a healthy diet and exercise regularly. For other teachers, management and organization are like starting an exercise program; they dedicate themselves to it in the beginning and then slack off until issues dictate action. For these teachers, common times of increased attention to classroom management are the starting and ending of school as well as near holidays which coincide with school breaks. Novice teachers, in particular, may try a variety of classroom management strategies to discover what works best for both their students and them, much like someone trying out different fitness classes at a new gym. A key to both a healthy lifestyle and a healthy classroom is consistency of effective actions.

> "Managing students in a way that creates a smoothly operating learning environment involves a series of highly fluid and dynamic teacher actions."[4]

What Do Researchers Say About the Learning Environment and Teacher Effectiveness?

When the learning environment is well-managed, the teacher proactively invests time and energy into creating a learning situation where students understand both what is expected of them as well as how to meet or exceed the expectations.[5] If a teacher has designed a classroom where issues are not addressed until they arise, then a more reactive climate exists in which time and effort are expended in addressing behavioral concerns.[6] Proactive management[7] of a classroom is characterized by:

- Teacher "withitness."
- Multitasking—keeping their eyes on more than one activity at a time.
- Varied and challenging independent work.
- Establishment of classroom rules and efficient routines.
- High standards for behavior along with positive personal interactions with students.
- Excellent organizational skills.

An astute teacher manages the instructional environment through coordination of instructional groups, transitions, and resources which results in increased teacher effectiveness.[8] Figure 4.1 provides a sample of research regarding the learning environment.

Figure 4.1. Findings Relating Learning Environment and Teacher Effectiveness

Major Findings	Study
Effective teachers spend more time at the start of the school year practicing and establishing classroom norms.	Emmer, Evertson, & Anderson, 1980
An exploratory study of third grade teachers found that in a sixty-minute period, ineffective teachers had, on average, five disruptive events occur compared to less than one for effective teachers.	Stronge, Ward, Tucker, & Hindman, 2008
Effective teachers clearly communicate expectations, provide examples of appropriate behavior, often post the rules or give students written copies of the rules, and approach the communication and teaching of behavioral requirements with the same care as they do teaching the content.	Gettinger & Kohler, 2006
A survey of 400 inner-city, low-income secondary students found that these learners perceived good teachers as those who controlled the classroom.	Corbett & Wilson, 2002
Students appreciate when teachers reinforce classroom requirements in a fair and respectful manner. Furthermore, students resent punitive correction resulting in public humiliation.	Hoy & Weinstein, 2006
The classroom learning environment can influence students' perspectives on learning. A student's sense of belonging to a class has been linked to students being more engaged in learning and being more motivated to perform in school.	Walker & Greene, 2009
A study found that classroom management was a significant predictor of students' reading and language scores on the Stanford 9.	Fidler, 2002

What Does the Learning Environment Convey When Nobody is There?

When the school year starts, teachers come into shells that most likely contain chalkboards/whiteboards, furniture, window shades, and equipment such as an overhead projector or computer. In the frenzied week before students arrive, teachers begin to transform the shells into stimulating environments. Once the students return, the shells evolve into dynamic classrooms containing hundreds of daily interactions. Effective teachers design a working environment to suit the instructional and developmental needs of their students.[9] Yet, when the classroom's occupants have gone home and the lights are turned out, what does the classroom's organization indicate about how it is managed and used? Furniture arrangement, classroom displays, and materials organization provide insight into how teachers and students use the space.[10] Figure 4.2 asks questions intended to promote reflection about one's classroom.

Figure 4.2. Empty Classroom Insights

Materials Organization	
How accessible are supplies that students routinely need?	◆ Materials are at an appropriate height. ◆ Items are freely available. For example, if a stapler is on the teacher's desk, students will often ask for permission to use it, which can be disruptive. This can be avoided by providing a stapler in a communally accessible area.
To what degree are supplies organized?	◆ Materials are arranged in containers by type, class, or activity. ◆ Containers may be color-coded by student group in elementary classrooms so that the group gets the same crayons, glue, markers, etc., back each time, which promotes better care of the items.
What safety precautions are evident in the room?	◆ The map of the building evacuation routes is posted in the event of fire/drill. ◆ Tornado and lockdown procedures are available. ◆ Science classrooms may have fire extinguishers, glass buckets, goggles, lab aprons, eye wash stations, and posted lab safety rules. ◆ Physical education classes may have first-aid kits if a school clinic is not available.
Room Arrangement	
How is movement facilitated in the room?	◆ "Avoid dead spaces and racetracks."[11] These spaces occur when movement is channeled by the placement of furniture and/or instructional materials. ◆ Adequate space exists for the teacher to circulate around the room to monitor students' work.[12]
What type of learning scenarios likely occur in the classroom?	◆ Desk arrangements in rows and columns are ideal for independent work and presentations. Horizontal rows facilitate working in pairs as well.[13] ◆ Clusters of desks or use of tables facilitate discussion and group activities. ◆ Centers provide students with opportunities to engage in learning as the teacher circulates.

How Does Cultural Responsiveness Relate to a Positive Learning Environment?

Everyday, teachers are anticipating the needs of their students. Working with diverse learners, whether the diversity is socioeconomic, cultural, or some other category, involves issues of safety, identity, language, culture, and ethnicity. Teachers of English language learners are often attuned to students' educational and cultural differences, but as classrooms become more reflective of a fluid and global society, all teachers need to be culturally responsive to meet the needs of students in order to create a positive classroom atmosphere. Increasingly, classrooms have diverse students for whom the following applies:

- ♦ Eye contact with authority figures is disrespectful, yet many teachers associate eye contact with honesty and being forthcoming; and

- ♦ Loud voices are conversations, yet for many teachers this may be construed as yelling.

A teacher's awareness of the cultural diversity within the classroom can lead to *understandings* that prevent *misunderstandings*.

An in-depth study of thirteen urban teachers in seven U.S. cities found that caring about students, acting with assertiveness and authority, and listening were keys to creating a productive and cooperative classroom environment.[14] Culturally responsive classroom management considers individual perspectives while maintaining high expectations for achievement and behavior (see, for example, "6 Responsive Behaviors" below).

6 Responsive Behaviors

An article[15] that specifically addressed culturally responsive classroom management and organization noted the importance of the following:

- ♦ Creating the learning environment—Have diverse images of people displayed in the classroom, acknowledge events/holidays celebrated by students, and arrange desks in clusters to promote interaction.

- ♦ Establishing behavioral expectations—Use explicitly stated rules that are modeled, practiced, and consistently reinforced.

- ♦ Communicating in culturally sensitive ways—Know the discourse patterns of the students as well as some of the common discontinuities in literal translations. For example, a teacher asks a student if he understands a question. The student responds "yes." The teacher thinks the student understands, but the student, by saying yes, is saying "I'm listening."

- ♦ Caring in the classroom—Demonstrate caring by greeting students at the door and inquiring about students' outside interests.

- ♦ Working with caregivers—Try to gain information about families' expectations for students, build trust with families, and garner their support for instructional efforts.

♦ Dealing with behavior problems—Consider the issue within its cultural context and develop constructive options. If the behavior is appropriate in the student's culture, then a disconnect exists between the current setting and the student's past experiences. A bridge of understanding needs to be constructed so that the student can alter his or her classroom behavior without embarrassment or shame.

How Can Rules and Routines Contribute to a Positive Learning Environment?

By Developing Rules and Routines

Classroom rules, routines, and norms are opportunities to clearly define the playing field for students and teachers. Providing students with opportunities to participate in these rules and routines increases their ownership in the classroom. An example is involving students in the attendance routine by having them move their picture into the "here" category each morning. This gives students some shared responsibility in the attendance process.[16] Another example is using student-created classroom rules, which could even be governed to a degree by the students themselves. For example, a teacher may reward students for following the classroom rules, but a peer also may nominate a student to receive recognition for being a good citizen based on a specific example. Additionally, a teacher could begin the year with bare classroom walls and have the students help to decorate the room when they arrive and participate in the decision-making process of how the room will be organized and the routines that will be followed. However, before all this can happen, a teacher needs to know her students and the students need to trust the teacher. Carefully scaffolded experiences to build capacity (see sidebar) aid in creating a productive and beneficial learning environment.

> **Building Capacity**
> ♦ Provide guidance for students about how to make good rules (e.g., number, clarity of the statement, stated positively, and—if possible—observable and measurable).[17]
>
> ♦ Hold short meetings at the start of the school year.[18]
>
> ♦ Model throughout the process using the guidelines for one rule and then guiding students to be the facilitators for other rules.

By Communicating Rules and Routines

Routines are a part of life from pregame rituals to brushing your teeth before going to bed. They provide a sense of control and direction and, therefore, help reduce stress and uncertainty. Routines go by a variety of names, such as procedures, regulations, guidance, and practices. Effective teachers use routines to reduce transition time, increase instructional time, and enhance the flow of the classroom. Once taught, routines are reinforced and feedback given to students as necessary to ensure smooth and efficient use of the routine. Thinking about how students and teachers function in the classroom can give rise to a need to change a routine. Likewise, providing clear, written explanations of routines can do the following:

- Help novice teachers think about and establish classroom routines.

- Assist teachers who need help with classroom management.

- Reaffirm the behaviors of teachers who use classroom routines to establish an efficiently run classroom so that they can share their "secrets of success" with others.

- Provide substitute teachers with the "classroom-based operational knowledge" necessary to maintain consistency.

- Serve as a reference (1) to orient new students arriving later in the year to class procedures or (2) for a student who has difficulty recalling how to sequence tasks.

By Following Through on Rules and Routines

In sports there are judges or referees who interpret the quality of play and ensure that the rules are followed. Sometimes students actively monitor the class norms and remind each other of expectations. From time to time, a teacher may solicit support in maintaining acceptable learner behavior from other colleagues or from the student's family. But ultimately it is the teacher who is responsible for discipline and the learners who are responsible for their behavioral choices. However, there are facets of discipline that can be addressed more effectively. Studies have found that the need for reprimands can be reduced if positive praise is used.[19] On the other hand, a 2008 Dutch study comparing the brain's responses to feedback found that eight- to nine-year-olds responded strongly to positive feedback while two older groups (eleven- to thirteen-year-olds, eighteen- to twenty-five-year-olds) had more active brains when negative feedback was used.[20] Thus, teachers must take into account the developmental level of the students when giving feedback. Consider these tips when making and enforcing rules:

- As feedback is given, try to consider the root cause of the behavior. Often misbehavior is the result of the student trying to get or avoid something. The rule infraction may be a symptom of the actual problem. By identifying the issue, the teacher can adequately address the problem or give an appropriate redirection.

- Make the rules and routines easy to follow. Provide adequate time for tasks and transitions. Let students know what their options are if work is finished quickly, assistance is needed, or time is a concern.

- Monitor progress, give specific praise, and correct errors.[21]

In summary, have clear and consistent expectations.

What Routines Are Important to Communicate?

Developing routines takes time, and many routines begin at the start of the school year. If a function happens frequently, there is often a routine attached to it such as getting ready for dismissal. A pair of authors[22] suggested that routines may be classified in four ways (see Figure 4.3).

Figure 4.3. Routine Classification

Type	What the Routine Does	Example
Activity	Facilitates student movement and transitions, such as getting into reading groups, going to centers, and moving into small groups for discussions	The teacher cues the students for the activity, and the students who were previously taught what to do take the appropriate actions.
Instructional	Applies to particular instructional strategies or methods	The first time a strategy is used, the teacher provides instruction on the strategy itself so that the next time the strategy is used only a verbal cue is needed.
Management	Supports the functioning of the classroom	Examples include taking attendance, turning in papers, getting needed materials, and participating in emergency drills (e.g., fire drills, tornado drills, etc.).
Executive Planning	Makes the teacher more efficient in his or her work	This is the teacher's process of approaching his or her work, such as reviewing last year's lesson plans to adapt them for the current year's learners.

The *Routine Memo* in Figure 4.4 is a tool that teachers may use to explain and record how the classroom functions for a substitute teacher or others.

Student Ownership

Why Does Student Ownership and Involvement Matter?

Suggestions in education literature offer multiple ways to give students ownership of their learning, from instruction to the creation of classroom rules.[23] Involving students in running the classroom makes them partners in their learning. Teachers begin the school year with different perspectives. Some teachers implement the rather unfortunate adage "don't let them see you smile the first week" and are overly strict. Other teachers begin the year with a series of experiences designed to get to know their students both as people and as learners while acclimating them to the teacher's expectations. The reality is that not everyone is ready to dive into student ownership; some of us prefer to wade in or dip our toes before we take the plunge.

Figure 4.4. Sample Completed Routine Memo

Tips for writing down routines
Think about how the routine works or will work
Compose thoughts sequentially
Use a series of *teacher actions* and *student actions* to indicate what each does
Tell information unique to the routine (e.g., cue word, helper's name)

This is how class starting activities (e.g., attendance, HW check, etc.) are done.

The following activities take 3-5 minutes to complete in total

Before Class – Teacher Action: Place any papers that need to be distributed to the class in the class bin. Write the starter activity on the whiteboard next to the construction paper label.

Class Change – Teacher Action: Stand in the doorway so that both the class and the hallway can be monitored. Greet students as they arrive.

Student Action: Upon entering the classroom each morning,
• students place their homework on the corner of their desks
• begin working on the starter activity that is written on the board

Taking Attendance and HW Check – Teacher Action: After students arrive, walk around the room with the attendance roster. Place a dot in the space next students' names when the student is present and has completed homework. If the student is absent, leave the space blank. If the student is present and does not have his or her homework, write a capital letter "O" in the box. Students know that they can bring assignments in later for credit. If a student happens to give you an additional assignment, place it in the substitute folder. (I will update the record later by coloring in the appropriate "O".)

Distributing Papers – Student Action: A designated student (whose name is on the job board) retrieves papers from the bin and passes them out to classmates. This student may be excused from the starter activity.

Discussing the Starter Activity – Teacher Action: Have students report their findings in a manner appropriate to the activity.

How Can Student Ownership Be Encouraged?

One way that student ownership can be encouraged is through the development of a classroom mission statement. Benefits[24] of a classroom mission statement include:

♦ Fostering discussion of what is important.

♦ Clarifying purpose.

♦ Helping reduce conflict between means and ends.

♦ Directing attention to values and culture.

There is widespread use of district- and schoolwide mission statements, but rarely are classroom mission statements found hanging on classroom walls. Yet, when asked, teachers often readily articulate what they want for their students. For example, a middle school science teacher shared what she wanted for her students when she responded to a parent inquiry about what she wanted for her students:

> I want my students to be confident in their science knowledge and skills. When I was sixteen, I participated in a field biology summer course for high schoolers taught by a college professor. As a college sophomore, when I saw an interesting senior/graduate-level class offered, I felt confident enough to ask the professor if I could enroll. I was admitted to the class and earned an A−. The grade isn't important, but it illustrates that when students experience science, they learn more than just content and how to use lab tools; they gain confidence in their abilities, which translates into opportunities later in life. I want my students to gain experiences that will not only prepare them for their next science class, but also for the future.

In essence, the science teacher was communicating her classroom mission, but it was lost in the long response.

Writing the mission statement down and sharing it with students, families, and school staff creates a focus for the instruction that occurs in each unique classroom setting. If the teacher above wrote a mission statement based on her response to the inquiry, it might read as follows:

> Mrs. Erlenmeyer is committed to the academic success of all her students through the use of hands-on and minds-on science experiences that unite real-world situations with the learning that occurs in the classroom in order to prepare learners to be successful and contributing members in future academic and real-world endeavors.

That is, the teacher identified the *means* as using experiences to bring the real world into the classroom in order to obtain the *ends* of having learners who were successful in future in-school and out-of-school situations.

The example also illustrates the power of teacher dispositions (see Chapter 2 for further discussion) as when the teacher was a student she experienced several positive dispositions from her teacher and wants to continue them with her students. A study found that positive teacher dispositions towards students were predictive of student self-determination, further the teacher quality and student treatment by the teacher were the teacher dispositions that were the stronger predictors.[25] The next step would be to have students contribute to the classroom mission statement.

The benefits[26] of a classroom mission statement are that it:

♦ Fosters discussion of what is important.

♦ Clarifies purpose.

♦ Helps reduce conflict between means and ends.

♦ Directs attention to values and culture.

Involving students in writing a classroom mission statement can be an opportunity to build the classroom community since developing a mission statement encourages students to "share ownership for their learning."[27] Consider the possibilities if our fictional teacher, Mrs. Erlenmeyer, had shared her mission and then asked the students about their goals for the class. A simple T-chart with means and ends would have helped students organize their thoughts for a classroom mission statement that might have read:

> Using investigative skills, our intelligence, and our ability to learn, we, the students of Mrs. Erlenmeyer's class, will demonstrate our excellence on the state test and dominate the science fair as we prepare to apply our learning to future science classes and our understanding of the world around us.

What Does a Classroom Mission Specify?

♦ Who is executing the mission.

♦ What needs exist or which issues need to be addressed.

♦ How the classroom occupants respond to needs and issues.

♦ The outcomes of the actions of the classroom occupants.

See the sidebar with a description of what a mission statement should specify.

How Can a Teacher Quickly Solicit Student Input?

Figures 4.5 (page 60) and 4.6 (page 61) contain surveys, one for younger students (Figure 4.5) and one for older students (Figure 4.6). The focus of both versions is to solicit information from students about their learning needs and classroom environmental preferences, and also to gain insight into what the student took away from last year's class in the same subject. While an effective teacher would conduct a more extensive preassessment of their students' learning, this survey is a casual way to get some information about what the student knows.

The survey in Figure 4.5 is for younger students who may need the survey read to them; students are asked to color the face that shows how they feel about each statement. Once the students have completed the surveys, it is time to review their answers to learn information about the learners. In Figure 4.5, a teacher has compiled the results of her students' survey response directly onto an extra copy of the survey. In examining the responses, questions 3 and 4 seem contradictory upon first glance, as students like

(Text continues on page 62.)

Figure 4.5. Sample Completed Student Survey

Name: _____

Color the face that shows how much you agree with the sentence.

1. So far today, I am having a good day at school.

| 15 | 5 | 2 |

2. I like math.

| 17 | 4 | 1 |

3. I like doing school work by myself.

| 22 | 0 | 0 |

4. I like working in groups.

| 14 | 5 | 3 |

5. I like talking about what I am learning.

| 19 | 3 | 0 |

6. I like doing activities to learn new things.

| 22 | 0 | 0 |

7. I like reading to learn new things.

| 4 | 13 | 5 |

8. I like listening to people tell me new things.

| 9 | 9 | 4 |

9. I like where I am sitting in the classroom right now.

| 14 | 5 | 3 |

10. I like it when the classroom is a little noisy.

| 15 | 1 | 6 |

Figure 4.6 Reproducible Resource: Student Survey

Student Survey

Name: _____ Class/Period: _____

This is not a graded assignment; however, it contains important information, so I will record that you turned it in completed. If you need more room, use the back of the paper or attach additional sheets.

1. Why are you taking this class?

2. What do you want to get out of this class?

3. What was the favorite or most interesting thing you learned in _____ (write in subject) class last year?

4. Share with me something you learned last year in _____(write in subject) that related to your life.

5. If your backpack could describe you, what would it say?

6. Tell me something that I should know about you as a *learner* and something you want me to know about you as a *person*.

   Learner

   Person

7. There are 24 hours in a day. Since everyone in the class sleeps and attends school, an average of 8 hours a night was used for sleep and an average of 9 hours was used for school (getting ready, trans portation to/from, and time at school). Finish the pie chart for how you spend the rest of your day (*include labels*).

8. If you could write the tests for this class, would they be:
   Check all question types that would be on your test
   ☐ True/false   ☐ Essay
   ☐ Multiple choice   ☐ Short answer
   ☐ Fill in the blank

9. Circle the degree to which you like to learn by the doing the five items below.

Reading	like it	neutral	do not like it
Doing/Hands-on	like it	neutral	do not like it
Listening	like it	neutral	do not like it
Discussing	like it	neutral	do not like it
Moving/Acting	like it	neutral	do not like it

10. Rank order the following 1-3, with #1 being your first choice and #3 being your last choice for how you like to work?
    ____Working in teams
    ____Working with a partner
    ____Working by myself

11. Where do you prefer to sit in the classroom?
    ☐ up front   ☐ in the middle   ☐ in the back
    ☐ other (tell me) _____

12. Classrooms can be loud or quiet, draw an arrow to indicate the noise level you are comfortable learning in most of the time.

Quiet	Low	Moderate	Bustling	Noisy	Loud
Almost no sound	Some sound	Some discussion and sounds of people moving like a classroom "hum"	Noise from several sources, so the classroom "buzzes"	Everyone is working and talking at once	Can not hear the person next to you talking

to work by themselves (question 3) and in groups (question 4), but the students are simply saying they like both. Overwhelmingly, these students prefer doing and interacting (questions 5 and 6) to learning new material through books. Depending on the age of the students, this may be a factor of their reading level. The responses to questions 6 and 10 are interesting because students indicated that they like talking while they learn (question 6), but six students indicated that they did not like a classroom that was a little noisy (question 10). Figure 4.6 shows the survey for older students with tips on what to look for in the responses. (Blank reproducible *Student Surveys* are available in Part II.)

Time Management

Why Does Time Matter?

"Teachers who effectively manage time give their students the best opportunity to learn and develop personal habits that lead to wise use of their time."[28] Effective teachers learn strategies and routines, refine lessons, and judiciously allocate their time so that the demands of their profession balance with their lives outside of school. Figure 4.7 illustrates four kinds of school time[29] and three types of timesavers[30] that ideally should balance with teacher time. At times the balance tips one way or the other, but for the most part it stays level. Using school time wisely is a hallmark of effective teachers, not only from the perspective of the task (e.g., instruction versus giving directions) but also the quality of the task.[31]

Figure 4.7. Professional and Teacher Time

School Time
- Allocated Time (what is assigned during the school day)
- Instructional Time (when the teacher is teaching)
- Engaged Time (when students are involved)
- Academic Learning Time (when students demonstrate learning)

Time-Saver Routines
- Activity-related (students are trained to do a task on cue, such as move into groups)
- Instruction-related (students are taught instructional strategies to use that, once learned, do not require explanations)
- Management-related (reduce administrative and transition time)

Teacher Time
- Family
- Home
- Shopping
- Housekeeping
- Friends
- Recreational activities
- Leisure activities
- Add your own_____
- _____
- _____
- _____
- _____
- _____
- _____
- _____
- _____
- _____
- _____
- _____
- _____

Why Does Time Management Matter?

Quality time matters more than seat time. Effective teachers are better at time management than their less-effective counterparts.[32] How teachers and schools use their allocated time has important implications for the success of the students, teachers, and schools, as is shown in Figure 4.8.

Figure 4.8. The Positive Impact of Well-Used Time

Major Findings	Study
Effective teachers actively manage the allocated class time to emphasize academics and minimize disruptions.	Covino & Iwanicki, 1996
Expert teachers are more efficient in using classroom time as they make use of routines, engaging instruction, and feedback to students in order to maximize time usage.	Cruickshank & Haefele, 2001
Schools with less than a ten-percentile gap between groups of students used time more effectively than schools with larger gaps. For example, teachers provided more opportunities for student-led activities (fifty-eight more hours per year).	Meehan, Cowley, Schumacher, Hauser, & Croom, 2003
Teachers who wait a few seconds after asking a question have more students who volunteer to respond and student-to-student interaction increases.	Cotton, 2001
Schools with large achievement gaps (greater than ten-percentile points), had teachers who spent more time on administrative tasks (twenty-four more hours over the course of a year).	Meehan, Cowley, Schumacher, Hauser, & Croom, 2003
Effective classroom mangers spent less time on transitions between activities than their less-effective colleagues, thus leaving more time for instruction.	Doyle, 1986

What Is the Value of Teacher Time?

Study after study has shown that teachers spend many noncontract hours working on school-related tasks (see sidebar "Time Use: Teachers vs. Business Managers" on page 64 for an example).[33] Some teachers seem to live and breathe education, working over and above their contract hours by putting in as many as sixty-five hours or more per week. In this case, the teacher has ceded part of his or her life to the school. Perhaps the teacher is new to the profession and is struggling to address the complex demands of the job, in which case the tipped scale is usually temporary. In reality, teachers cannot sustain such a pace over the long-term. Such a demanding pace, itself, creates a lot of stress on the teacher, which is only compounded by the demands of the job. Indeed, when teachers' estimates of their time use were compared to time diaries, researchers found that teachers underestimated their workload.[34] The intrinsic rewards of teaching

Time Use: Teachers vs. Business Managers

A Canadian time-use study comparing teachers to business managers/administrators found that teachers are busier, experience more stress, and enjoy their work more than the comparison group with a comparable level of education.[35] Furthermore, the study found that female teachers perceive more stress than their male counterparts. Teachers reported feeling rushed and stressed in the performance of their work. On average, teachers spent twenty-one more minutes during a weekday and fifty-nine more minutes during a weekend day at home working on work-related activities than did managers. Teachers do not seem to have an accurate sense of how much time they spend working outside of the classroom.

can be motivating, but the stress of teaching can also be high, and balancing time can be a challenge.

When time use is discussed in relationship to what effective teachers do, it refers to the use of school time. However, the teacher's time should not be ignored. With the majority of teachers being female, important gender differences come to light. "Generally research shows…women spend more time than men on domestic work. Men also spend twice as much time as women on sports and hobbies."[36] Given that male and female teachers in the study spent comparable amounts of time on school-related work, what they did with their teacher or personal time is noteworthy. Interestingly, women were not engaged in stress-relieving activities to the same degree as their male counterparts. When discussing time use, it is critical to remember that personal time is a necessity, not a luxury.

How Can a Teacher Determine Time Use?

Time in a school day is finite. Before students even enter the building The clock has started ticking for teachers as they rush around taking care of last-minute preparations. And when students leave at the end of the day, the pace continues. Research corroborates what educators already know: Some teachers are better at managing time than others.[37]

In some ways, minutes in the classroom are like dollars in your wallet—they just seem to disappear. When you stop to think of how the time or the cash was spent, major expenditures are recalled, but the small costs are often lost. By recording time on a log, the time is not lost but rather becomes a focus for reflection. Some activities take longer than others. The *Time Use Log* in Figure 4.9 is designed to capture a snapshot of how teachers are using their allocated time. (A blank reproducible template of the *Time Use Log* is available in Part II.) By examining several days of time use, patterns emerge that can inform professional practice.

Observing with the Time Use Log

How much time is necessary to determine a pattern in time use? The quick answer is "it depends." A one-day snapshot may be quite telling. However, if possible, collect three to six days of observations so that patterns can be seen. How the information is gathered is equally important as how many days of observation capture time use data. There are several ways to collect the information on the *Time Use Log*:

Figure 4.9. Sample Completed Time Use Log

Directions: Start from the bottom, and with each new use of time draw a line across the column. In the space between the two lines, indicate what occurred in the classroom.

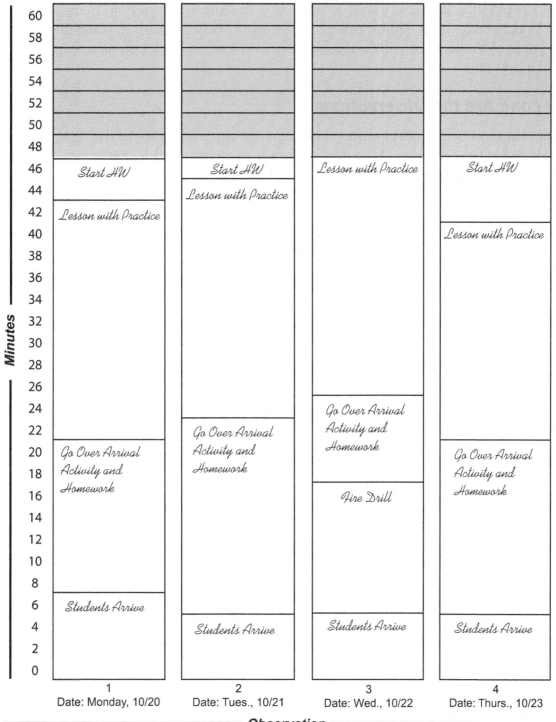

- Recording a class on videotape to analyze later.

- Inviting a colleague to conduct several observations (and then returning the professional courtesy).

- Keeping the log handy so that with each transition it is easy to mark what is occurring. *Note:* This approach is the most likely to result in some missed time as the teacher will be focused more on teaching than on recording the activities.

How Long Are the Observations?

The duration of the observation time depends on what activity the teacher wants to analyze for time savings. Take, for example, a teacher who is concerned about the amount of time it takes to collect homework. This teacher could record on the *Time Use Log* her start and end times for collecting homework by subject for several days in order to get an average. Such a simple application does not require a form or even an external way to observe. But more than likely, a teacher may want an entire lesson segment observed. This may mean a twenty-five-minute handwriting lesson or a forty-two-minute mathematics class, or perhaps a ninety-minute foreign language class. By observing the entire lesson, the teacher can see how the time is used during different segments of the class. Similarly, the teacher likely will identify areas to conserve time in order to reallocate it to other needs.

How Is the Time Use Log Used?

The time-use log is a stacked bar graph in which the observer starts at the bottom (zero minutes) and makes a line when the target activity transitions to something else. In the space between the two lines, a notation is made as to how the time was used. This continues for the entire observation. Individuals who are very visual may want to use different colors to denote specific activities.

Reflecting with the Time Use Log

A teacher who has recorded information on the *Time Use Log* will want to consider if the time use matches the perception of how time flows during class, including how the chunks of allocated time are used. Questions to ask include:

- How much time is spent on instructional versus noninstructional activities (e.g., taking attendance, packing up for the next class)?

- What types of activities are the students doing?

- What is unexpected in the observation of time use?

Imagine being in a forty-six-minute Algebra II mathematics class that ran like clockwork (see Figure 4.9, page 65), with fifteen minutes on homework review, twenty minutes on the new material, and the remaining time spent on starting the next day's homework or packing up. Some would say that the teacher's time use is remarkably consistent—even with a fire drill on Day 3. Others might express concern that the regularity suggests that the teacher delivers material without responding to students' needs. With just a graph, only part of the story is told; the rest depends on context. The *Time Use Log* is not intended as a standalone tool. Rather, it serves as an information source about what typically occurs.

Summary

Teaching and learning is the basis for our educational system and is at the core of what teachers in classrooms do every day. However, a teacher's skill in developing engaging lessons, implementing high expectations during the lesson, and creating appropriate assessments, are supported by the teacher's skill in ensuring that the classroom functions efficiently and effectively. The seamless and smooth functioning of the classroom is contingent upon whether a positive learning environment exists, whether instructional time is maximized, and how valued students feel in the learning process.

Notes

1   Barbetta, Norona, & Bicard, 2005, p. 17.

2   Lewis, 2004.

3   Covino & Iwanicki, 1996; Wang, Haertel, & Walberg, 1993.

4   Brown, 2003, p. 281.

5   Zahorik, Halbach, Ehrle, & Molnar, 2003.

6   Brophy, 2000.

7   Bain, & Jacobs, 1990; Covino & Iwanicki, 1996; Good & Brophy, 1997; Marzano, 2003.

8   Danielson, 1996.

9   Kohn, 1996.

10 Stronge, 2007.

11 Hoy & Hoy, 2003, p. 200.

12 McLeod, Fisher, & Hoover, 2003.

13 Hoy & Hoy, 2003.

14 Brown, 2003.

15 Weinstein, Curran, & Tomlinson-Clarke, 2003.

16 Good, 2005.

17 Barbetta, Norona, & Bicard, 2005.

18 Barbetta et al., 2005.

19 Swinson & Harrop, 2005; vanDuijenvoorde, Zanolie, Rombouts, Raijamerks, & Crone, 2008.

20 vanDuijenvoorde, et al., 2008.

21 Conroy, Sutherland, Snyder, & Marsh, 2008.

22 Burden & Byrd, 1994.

23 Enghag & Niedderer, 2008; Kentish, 1995; Platz, 1994.

24 Bryson, 1995.

25 Hong & Shull, 2009.

26 Bryson, 1995.

27 Thiede, 2002, p. 10.

28 McLeod, Fisher, & Hoover, 2003, ¶26.

29 Wong & Wong, 1998.

30 Burden & Byrd, 1994.

31 Foorman, Schatschneider, Eakin, Fletcher, Moats, & Francis, 2006.

32 Cruickshank & Haefele, 2001.

33 Michelson & Harvey, 2000; Prisoners of Time, 1994.

34 Naylor, 2001.

35 Michelson & Harvey, 2000.

36 Naylor, 2001, p. 9.

37 Cruickshank & Haefele, 2001.

5

Conclusion

How can we best support teaching and learning? There are myriad ways to answer this question, from rhetorical to pragmatic. Throughout *The Supportive Learning Environment: Effective Teaching Practices* we have built a bridge between research and practice on essential attributes that do, in fact, support quality teaching and student success. In this concluding chapter for Part I, we follow a different path in emphasizing how we can support teacher quality. Specifically, we emphasize the roles of school leaders and teachers, themselves, in building success; we then turn our attention to how teacher quality supports our ultimate educational goal—student success. The following questions relate to how and why we can and should provide the proper support mechanisms for teachers and students:

♦ How can principals support teacher effectiveness?

♦ How can teachers support their own quality?

♦ How can teachers support student success?

How Can Principals Support Teacher Effectiveness Through School Culture?

Among all the responsibilities that are fulfilled by principals, sustaining teacher quality may be the most important and have the most lasting effect on the success of the school community.[1] As we well know, effective principals create a culture that fosters a sense of belonging among the entire faculty. In this culture, teachers are supported by mentoring programs and other meaningful professional development opportunities rather than left to flounder alone.

The terms "climate" and "culture" tend to be used in a highly interactive, if not interchangeable, fashion when discussing qualities of school success. One key difference between the two terms is based on the perspective or lens through which one is viewing the school context. Both climate and culture are concerned with the identity, feel, and tone of a school.[2] The difference between the two concepts is a matter of context. *Climate* is a psychologically influenced view of the quality of the school workplace experienced by the employees and affecting their behavior. *Culture* has its roots in anthropology and, when applied to schools, is concerned with accomplishing both academic goals and caring for students while acknowledging the disruptions that occur from outside the school's influence.

In studies of organizational climate and culture, student performance levels and perceived trust are higher in schools with higher scores on culture and climate instruments.[3] A healthy school climate has higher levels of employee satisfaction and more positive interactions between teachers and leadership. Teachers and administrators trust and rely upon each other. When teachers trust their leadership, they are more willing to take risks and share with others.[4]

A key facet to building a healthy climate is to maintain trust and if necessary to begin the painstaking process of building trust. According to Tschannen-Moran, "Even when school leaders work to build a common vision and foster acceptance of group goals, without trust these leaders do not inspire their constituencies to go beyond minimum requirements."[5]

Most people—including most teachers—don't want to work where the environment feels toxic, depressing, or defeating. Rather, an environment that is positive, supportive, and growth promoting is more motivating and more likely leads to positive relationships in which the vision and mission of a school are realized. Thus, teacher quality is promoted in a real measure when principals and others support and help sustain healthy working conditions and learning environments. Student achievement is also promoted by this healthy state.

> **Climate and School Effectiveness**
>
> In a study, responses of ninety-eight Dutch principals, 858 of their students, and 637 of their teachers showed that a positive relationship exists between a principal's ability to maintain a strong school climate and that school's effectiveness. Further, the study found that the principal's vision impacted what the principal did; furthermore, teachers' perception of the school was related to principals' instructional leadership.[6]

How Can Teachers Support Their Own Quality?

What is the Role of Reflection in Improving Teacher Performance?

Teacher reflection is an auditing process of sorts in which teachers consciously and crucially analyze their actions and beliefs. As teachers develop from novices to experts, they typically gain fluidity in their actions as some tasks—such as swiftly quelling a potential disruption with a quick glance—become almost automated, allowing the teacher to focus instead on instructional and student issues.

Classroom teaching is often like being in the fast lane of a freeway with lots of changes. Just as a driver with a car on cruise control continues to pay attention to the road, a teacher using established routines to enhance the efficiency of the classroom is alert, always looking for the next opening for learning, speeding up and slowing down in response to the students' needs, and anticipating detours, roadblocks, and exits along the way.

> "Reflection is the 'supervisor' that encourages teachers to continue what worked and correct what isn't working."[7] It is a lifelong practice common to effective teachers.[8]

What Is the Basis of Teacher Reflection?

Rarely is an article on reflection written without a well-deserved nod to John Dewey who wrote in the 1930s that teacher's work was complex and involved a great deal of thinking. Many things in life replay through our minds and we analyze why an activity was such a success or how we could have done something better. In essence, we learn not only by doing, but also through thinking about what we did. Research on teacher reflection often discusses the reflective process used to develop subject matter and pedagogical knowledge, increase understanding of students, release frustrations, and improve professional practice. In essence, teacher reflection is a powerful means of supporting teacher development in a uniquely personal way.[9]

How Do Quality Teachers Reflect to Improve Their Professional Practice?

Many teachers who completed a teacher-preparation program were asked to discuss with their cooperating teacher or college supervisor their teaching practices. Unfortunately, once teachers are in their own classrooms, the necessity to critically analyze teaching practices and beliefs often diminishes as a formal practice as immediate challenges of addressing the curriculum and student needs takes precedence. Nonetheless, reflection can—and must—still occur as teachers think about their day and what needs to occur the next day.

Reflection is about critically considering issues that may be uncomfortable for teachers.[10] The practice takes on many forms. It may be a structured activity for preservice teachers who are asked to reflect on specific components of their developing professional practice or it may be a more cathartic experience. In collegial groups, teachers discuss, listen, and reflect on practices and situations that occur through the course of their work. Kathleen Sharp, a teacher with 28 years of teaching experience, wrote:

> Thinking deeply about my work has increased my effectiveness and allowed me to assist my students in learning. My constant reflection facilitates my thinking as I consider instructional materials, activities, and lessons I prepare and assign.[11]

Teacher reflection can be both *deliberate and formal*, as well as *incidental and informal* (Figure 5.1). In whatever form, it is essential that reflection occurs. After all, reflection is a critical attribute of quality teachers and an essential component of improving teaching quality.

Figure 5.1. Means of Teacher Reflection

Deliberate and Formal	Incidental and Informal
◆ Writing in journals ◆ Contributing regularly to a blog, Ning site, etc. ◆ Working with colleagues in professional learning communities	◆ During a brief moment between classes ◆ Right in the middle of a lesson as an "aha" insight reveals itself ◆ In a quiet moment driving home from work in the afternoon

How Can Teachers Support Student Success?

The Ultimate Test of Teacher Quality: Holding High, Reasonable Expectations for Students

In a well-known study conducted in the 1960s, teachers were told that one group of students they were teaching had high potential whereas another group of students did not have quite as impressive scores. In reality, however, the groups were switched so that the high-potential group was composed of the lower-achieving students and vice versa. In the end, the lower-achieving group of students whose teachers were told to expect a lot ended up performing well.[12]

The Rosenthal and Jacobson study described above was an example of a self-fulfilling prophecy; that is, based on advance information, teachers form expectations and act accordingly. A five-step model[13] illustrates how this works (Figure 5.2).

Figure 5.2. Model for Teacher Expectations and Student Learning

1. The teacher develops expectations based on available information.

2. The teacher acts based on these expectations.

3. The teacher communicates to the student what is expected behaviorally and/or academically.

4. The teacher (ideally) continues to steps 1 and 2 to shape the student's actions.

5. The student's actions over time are more aligned with the teacher's expectations.

Self-fulfilling prophecies have the potential to be both damaging and beneficial. If the teacher believes and communicates high expectations to students, students often respond favorably to the positive messages, support, and challenges that are offered at a level that is accessible to the student. The harmful side of self-fulfilling prophecies is when a teacher acts on stereotypes such as the school's reputation as being low achieving, negative comments about students, socioeconomic status, and so on. What makes the latter scenario especially problematic is that research has found that teachers who act on low expectations based on some of these factors often are not even aware of their biases and the impact on students.[14]

Translating High Expectations into Student Success

High expectations do not automatically translate into high-quality teacher classroom practices and increased student learning. Just having a conviction that students can achieve is far from enough. To actualize the connections between high expectations and student academic success, teachers need to carefully think about and plan what expectations look like in terms of concrete behaviors and learning outcomes, and enact them in real classrooms (Figure 5.3).

Figure 5.3. Sample Teacher Actions and Attributes Supporting Teaching and Learning

Action Item	Sample Teacher Action
Communication between teachers and students	♦ Articulating academic and behavior expectations ♦ Encouraging and involving students in discussion about the expectations ♦ Sharing expectations with students' families ♦ Ensuring that the teacher's actions reflect his or her expectations ♦ Providing feedback to students and their families about how students are meeting expectations
Striving for equity in classrooms	♦ Giving students attention, regardless of achievement levels. Researchers have noted that students at the top often receive more attention than students at the bottom of the class ♦ Setting expectations based on the student and supporting the student in meeting those expectations—indeed, one size *does not* fit all ♦ Becoming culturally competent ♦ Acknowledging and addressing your own biases
Focusing on the individual student	♦ Believing in your ability to make a positive difference for each student ♦ Interacting with students outside of the classroom—may be as simple as a telephone call home about a positive event in class or attending a band concert to show that you care about students as individuals ♦ Analyzing student data for needs and strengths to better tailor learning experiences ♦ Planning for the student by filling gaps in learning, using different strategies, and incorporating students' interests
Accepting responsibility for students' success	♦ Believing in yourself ♦ Setting high and appropriate expectations for students ♦ Requiring the best from students such as high-quality work and timely submission of work. Some schools have "no zero" policies so that teachers and students must be accountable for the work that is assigned. ♦ Monitoring student progress and providing feedback

Translating High Expectations into Daily Practice

Teachers who have high expectations for their students also hold themselves accountable for student success that challenges both themselves and their students to excel at a higher level. High expectations work when there is a resonance between the teachers' expectations and the support students receive. Without day-to-day teacher efforts within their classroom practices to convey their expectations, the students may not realize they are expected to achieve more. And without their input of effort, the distance between the status quo and the aspired status is unbridgeable. So how can high expectations become reality in a classroom? Actually, some little daily routines and behaviors that teachers cultivate and practice in their classrooms can become influential in communicating to students what they believe and expect. Figure 5.4 provides some examples. In the final analysis, teacher expectations have a powerful influence on what students learn do not learn in the classroom.

Figure 5.4. Little Things Pay Big Dividends

Do	Why
Know students' names	A survey of 225 urban high school seniors found that if teachers were "mean" and did not know students' names, students' tended to have negative impressions of teachers.[15]
Be polite	The teacher's attitude sets the tone.
Cultivate a community	Cultivate a sense of community increases a sense of responsibility, belonging, and self-discipline.
Monitor classroom timing	Observe the pace with which students work during instruction, have options available for students who finish accurately and quickly, intervene when students are struggling, and provide timely and targeted feedback. These actions promote good classroom behavior as student frustration is kept to a minimum and success is not only possible, but is recognized.[16]

Summary

The only justification for public (or private, for that matter) education to exist is to improve the quality of life of our students, and the primary way we do this is by helping them learn to read, to understand math, to appreciate the world around them, to be prepared to productively participate in their world, to live healthy and happy lives, and so forth. In other words, everything we do in education—*everything*—should positively touch the life of a child.[17]

As suggested above, our business is teaching and learning. One simple conclusion regarding effective teachers is abundantly clear: the common denominator in school improvement and student success *is* the teacher.[18] As we support teacher success in every reasonable fashion, we also support student success.

Notes

1   Stronge, Richard, & Catano, 2008.

2   Hoy, 2002.

3   Hoy, 2002.

4   Tschannen-Moran, 2004.

5   Tschannen-Moran, 2004, p. 174.

6   Krüger, et al., 2007.

7   Harris, 2003, p. 39.

8   Grossman, Valencia, Evans, Thompson, Martin, & Place, 2000; Thomas & Montomery, 1998.

9   Hindman, Stronge, & Tucker, 2003.

10   Hoffman-Kipp, Artiles, & López-Torres, 2003.

11   Sharp, 2003, p. 243.

12   Rosenthal and Jacobson, 1966.

13   Tauber, 1998.

14   Cotton, 1989.

15   Hoy & Weinstein, 2006.

16   Gettinger & Kohler, 2006.

17   Stronge & Grant, 2009.

18   Stronge, Ward, & Grant, 2008.

Part II
Reproducible Resources

Throughout the book, numerous tools have been presented relating to planning, teaching, and assessing students. Part II contains full-page blanks of the resources for purchasers of the book to copy for educational use and not-for-profit use. The resources are presented alphabetically. The matrix below provides a quick reference telling the title, the original figure number, a brief purpose, and the page number. Additionally notes relating to the use of the resource are provided as applicable.

Title	Fig. #	Purpose	Page #
Communication Observation Record	3.7	To facilitate guided reflection upon what a teacher said and how someone else responded, and to evaluate the outcome based on what the intended message was. There are times when an unintended message results in a need to examine what was said from the other party's perspective.	80
Immediacy Interaction Record	2.1	To facilitate an examination of a teacher's immediacy behaviors with students—both verbal and nonverbal.	81
Planning for Online Group Mentoring		To help expert teachers and educational leaders plan and create an effective virtual community to be used as a component of a mentoring program.	82
Professional Development Plan	3.9	To provide teachers a means to organize their professional development offerings in order to evaluate the best option for them. *Note:* This could be affixed to the inside of a file folder where the teacher places items of interest throughout the year to review for summer professional development or to save for sometime in the future.	83
Routine Memo	4.4	To record classroom routines that would be beneficial for a substitute teacher, classroom visitor, or new student to know.	84
Student Information Sheet	2.7	To gather information about how parents/caregivers prefer to be contacted, solicit information about the student, offer ways for the caregiver to become involved in the classroom, and serve as a future record of communications between school and home.	85
Student Surveys	4.5 4.6	To provide students an opportunity to share with their teachers how they like to learn and perceive learning. There is a lower elementary version and one appropriate for older students.	86 87
Student–Teacher Interactions	2.5	To offer insight on the teacher's behavior, both verbal and nonverbal, with students.	88
Time Use Form	4.9	To identify how class time is allocated.	89

Communication Observation Record

Teacher Said	Response	Meant
	☐ Complied ☐ Did not respond ☐ Adversarial verbal/ nonverbal language	Follow up to be done ☐ No ☐ Yes (specify)
	☐ Complied ☐ Did not respond ☐ Adversarial verbal/ nonverbal language	Follow up to be done ☐ No ☐ Yes (specify)
	☐ Complied ☐ Did not respond ☐ Adversarial verbal/ nonverbal language	Follow up to be done ☐ No ☐ Yes (specify)
	☐ Complied ☐ Did not respond ☐ Adversarial verbal/ nonverbal language	Follow up to be done ☐ No ☐ Yes (specify)

Immediacy Interaction Record

Teacher's Name _____ Observer's Name _____

Date _____ Time *start* _____ *end* _____

Directions: Observe the teacher and record each teacher immediacy–student interaction in the summary cells below using a tally mark. Interactions are tallied when they are specifically directed toward specific student(s). For example, "good morning class" is not tallied, whereas greeting a student by name is tallied.

Immediacy Summary

	Tally	Total
Verbal		
Feedback		
Greeting		
Positive comment/compliment		
Student life inquiry (e.g., sports, band, special event)		
Other—specify		
Nonverbal		
Eye contact		
Head nod		
Positive facial expression		
Smile		
Other—specify		

Planning for Online Group Mentoring

Online group mentoring is a type of virtual learning community. When conceptualizing and constructing such a community, several important questions must be answered. Use this tool to help in planning for and creating a professional learning community in a virtual environment so that it is *intentional* (i.e., serves the purposes of your organization), *constructive* (i.e., adds genuine value to the professional practice of teachers), and *feasible* (i.e., can be efficiently and effectively used within teachers' professional lives).

1. Will mentoring consist of group mentoring only, or will one-to-one mentoring also be a component?

2. Will mentoring consist of the online forum only, or will face-to-face mentoring also be a component?

3. Will online communications be asynchronous, synchronous, or both?

4. Will the community be open or closed?

5. Will the potential pool of mentors be local or geographically diverse?

6. How and by whom will *mentors* be trained in each of the following areas: mentoring skills, online protocol, and technical skills associated with the online forum?

7. How and by whom will *new teachers* be oriented to the group mentoring forum (e.g., purpose of forum, uses of the forum, online protocol, and technical skills associated with the forum)?

8. What role will the site facilitator or moderator play in group interactions?

9. What computer-mediated communication tools will be used in the online forum (e.g., e-mail, webcasts, voice, video, wiki, surveying/polling)?

10. What will be archived from the forum (e.g., usage/login data, webcasts, chats, threaded discussions)?

Professional Development Plan Template

Professional's Name:	Subject/Grade Level:	
Goal(s):		

Possible Steps/Strategies	Time Frame	Cost
☐ University/College Course Options:		
☐ Self-Study Options:		
☐ Summer Training Options:		
Final Decision:		

Routine Memo

Tips for writing down routines

Think about how the routine works or will work

Compose thoughts sequentially

Use a series of *teacher actions* and *student actions* to indicate what each does

Tell information unique to the routine (e.g., cue word, helper's name)

This is how _____ are done.

_____

_____

_____

_____

_____

_____

_____

_____

_____

_____

_____

_____

_____

_____

_____

_____

_____

_____

_____

_____

_____

_____

_____

_____

_____

_____

Student Information Sheet

Student Information Sheet

To be completed by the parent/caregiver

Student Name: _____

Parent/Caregiver Name(s): _____

Preferred Telephone Number to Use ☐ Home ☐ Work ☐ Cell _____

Email Address: _____

☐ *Check here if you would like to receive periodic updates of class assignments.*

How do you prefer that I contact you? *Check one:* ☐ Email ☐ Telephone ☐ Written Note

Please share with me talents or skills that you have that you would be willing to share with the class. *Check the box(es) below.*

☐ Volunteer outside of class
☐ Provide baked goods
☐ Collect materials that can be reused in class such as gallon milk jugs
   (teacher will contact to get specific items)
☐ Classroom volunteer working with students
☐ Classroom volunteer creating class materials
☐ Field trip chaperone
☐ Guest speaker – *tell area of interest* _____
☐ Other – *please tell how you would like to volunteer* _____

Tell me what I should know about your child as his/her teacher.

Does your student have any of the following on file with the school?
Check the box(es) ☐ Medical Alert (e.g., allergy)   ☐ IEP/504 Plan

(*Parents:* This portion of the form is for me to keep track of my communication with you
          throughout the year.)

Contact Log

Date	Purpose	Person	Mode
			☐ Email ☐ Meeting ☐ Note ☐ Telephone
			☐ Email ☐ Meeting ☐ Note ☐ Telephone
			☐ Email ☐ Meeting ☐ Note ☐ Telephone
			☐ Email ☐ Meeting ☐ Note ☐ Telephone

Please return this sheet to your student's teacher.

Student Survey I

Name: _____

Color the face that shows how much you agree with the sentence.

1. So far today, I am having a good day at school.

   😊 😐 ☹️

2. I like _____ (insert subject name).

   😊 😐 ☹️

3. I like doing school work by myself.

   😊 😐 ☹️

4. I like working in groups.

   😊 😐 ☹️

5. I like talking about what I am learning.

   😊 😐 ☹️

6. I like doing activities to learn new things.

   😊 😐 ☹️

7. I like reading to learn new things.

   😊 😐 ☹️

8. I like listening to people tell me new things.

   😊 😐 ☹️

9. I like where I am sitting in the classroom right now.

   😊 😐 ☹️

10. I like it when the classroom is a little noisy.

    😊 😐 ☹️

Student Survey II

1. Why are you taking this class?

2. What do you want to get out of this class?

3. What was the favorite or most interesting thing you learned in _____ (write in subject) class last year?

4. Share with me something you learned last year in _____(write in subject) that related to your life.

5. If your backpack could describe you, what would it say?

6. Tell me something that I should know about you as a *learner* and something you want me to know about you as a *person*.

   Learner

   Person

7. There are 24 hours in a day. Since everyone in the class sleeps and attends school, an average of 8 hours a night was used for sleep and an average of 9 hours was used for school (getting ready, trans portation to/from, and time at school). Finish the pie chart for how you spend the rest of your day (*include labels*).

8. If you could write the tests for this class, would they be:
   Check all question types that would be on your test
   ☐ True/false   ☐ Essay
   ☐ Multiple choice   ☐ Short answer
   ☐ Fill in the blank

9. Circle the degree to which you like to learn by the doing the five items below.

Reading	like it	neutral	do not like it
Doing/Hands-on	like it	neutral	do not like it
Listening	like it	neutral	do not like it
Discussing	like it	neutral	do not like it
Moving/Acting	like it	neutral	do not like it

10. Rank order the following 1-3, with #1 being your first choice and #3 being your last choice for how you like to work?
    ____Working in teams
    ____Working with a partner
    ____Working by myself

11. Where do you prefer to sit in the classroom?
    ☐ up front   ☐ in the middle   ☐ in the back
    ☐ other (tell me) _____

12. Classrooms can be loud or quiet, draw an arrow to indicate the noise level you are comfortable learning in most of the time.

Quiet	**Low**	**Moderate**	**Bustling**	**Noisy**	**Loud**
Almost no sound	Some sound	Some discussion and sounds of people moving like a classroom "hum"	Noise from several sources, so the classroom "buzzes"	Everyone is working and talking at once	Can not hear the person next to you talking

Student–Teacher Interactions

Nature of Teacher-to-Student Interactions

Teacher: _____ Number of Students: _____

Observation Date: _____ Start Time: _____ End Time: _____

Directions: Focus on the teacher's interactions with students. For each observed interaction, make two checkmarks, one to indicate the purpose for the interaction and the second to describe the tone of the interaction as positive, neutral, or negative. Then tally the number interactions related to behavior management and tone. Suggested observation is for 30 interactions. This is approximately 15 minutes.

KEY	
B when the purpose of the interaction is for Behavior Management	+ indicates positive/affirming/praise
I when the purpose of the interaction is for Instruction	N indicates neutral
F when the purpose of the interaction is for Feedback	- indicates negative/punitive
O is for "Other" which should be specified	

1	Purpose: ☐ B ☐ I ☐ F ☐ O Tone: ☐ + ☐ N ☐ -	16	Purpose: ☐ B ☐ I ☐ F ☐ O Tone: ☐ + ☐ N ☐ -
2	Purpose: ☐ B ☐ I ☐ F ☐ O Tone: ☐ + ☐ N ☐ -	17	Purpose: ☐ B ☐ I ☐ F ☐ O Tone: ☐ + ☐ N ☐ -
3	Purpose: ☐ B ☐ I ☐ F ☐ O Tone: ☐ + ☐ N ☐ -	18	Purpose: ☐ B ☐ I ☐ F ☐ O Tone: ☐ + ☐ N ☐ -
4	Purpose: ☐ B ☐ I ☐ F ☐ O Tone: ☐ + ☐ N ☐ -	19	Purpose: ☐ B ☐ I ☐ F ☐ O Tone: ☐ + ☐ N ☐ -
5	Purpose: ☐ B ☐ I ☐ F ☐ O Tone: ☐ + ☐ N ☐ -	20	Purpose: ☐ B ☐ I ☐ F ☐ O Tone: ☐ + ☐ N ☐ -
6	Purpose: ☐ B ☐ I ☐ F ☐ O Tone: ☐ + ☐ N ☐ -	21	Purpose: ☐ B ☐ I ☐ F ☐ O Tone: ☐ + ☐ N ☐ -
7	Purpose: ☐ B ☐ I ☐ F ☐ O Tone: ☐ + ☐ N ☐ -	22	Purpose: ☐ B ☐ I ☐ F ☐ O Tone: ☐ + ☐ N ☐ -
8	Purpose: ☐ B ☐ I ☐ F ☐ O Tone: ☐ + ☐ N ☐ -	23	Purpose: ☐ B ☐ I ☐ F ☐ O Tone: ☐ + ☐ N ☐ -
9	Purpose: ☐ B ☐ I ☐ F ☐ O Tone: ☐ + ☐ N ☐ -	24	Purpose: ☐ B ☐ I ☐ F ☐ O Tone: ☐ + ☐ N ☐ -
10	Purpose: ☐ B ☐ I ☐ F ☐ O Tone: ☐ + ☐ N ☐ -	25	Purpose: ☐ B ☐ I ☐ F ☐ O Tone: ☐ + ☐ N ☐ -
11	Purpose: ☐ B ☐ I ☐ F ☐ O Tone: ☐ + ☐ N ☐ -	26	Purpose: ☐ B ☐ I ☐ F ☐ O Tone: ☐ + ☐ N ☐ -
12	Purpose: ☐ B ☐ I ☐ F ☐ O Tone: ☐ + ☐ N ☐ -	27	Purpose: ☐ B ☐ I ☐ F ☐ O Tone: ☐ + ☐ N ☐ -
13	Purpose: ☐ B ☐ I ☐ F ☐ O Tone: ☐ + ☐ N ☐ -	28	Purpose: ☐ B ☐ I ☐ F ☐ O Tone: ☐ + ☐ N ☐ -
14	Purpose: ☐ B ☐ I ☐ F ☐ O Tone: ☐ + ☐ N ☐ -	29	Purpose: ☐ B ☐ I ☐ F ☐ O Tone: ☐ + ☐ N ☐ -
15	Purpose: ☐ B ☐ I ☐ F ☐ O Tone: ☐ + ☐ N ☐ -	30	Purpose: ☐ B ☐ I ☐ F ☐ O Tone: ☐ + ☐ N ☐ -

Totals

Behavior		Positive		Neutral		Negative	
Instruction		Positive		Neutral		Negative	
Feedback		Positive		Neutral		Negative	
Other		Positive		Neutral		Negative	
OVERALL		Positive		Neutral		Negative	

Comments

Time Use Log

Time Use Log

Directions: Start from the bottom, and with each new use of time draw a line across the column. In the space between the two lines, indicate what occurred in the classroom.

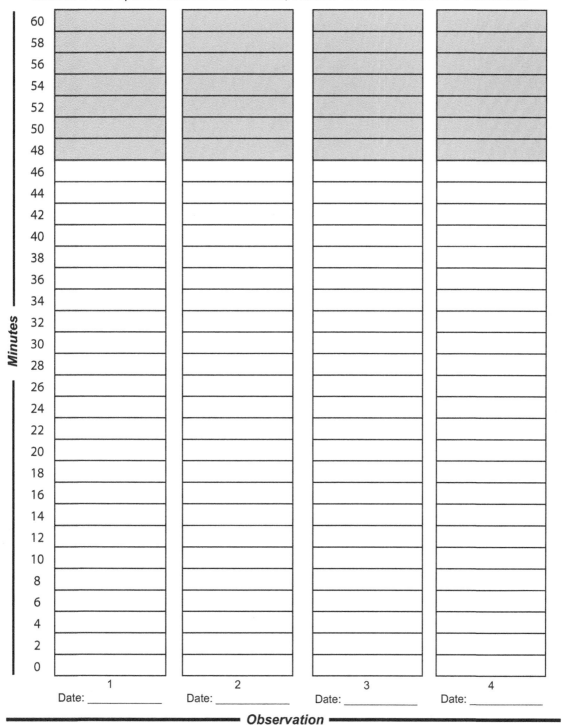

Minutes

60
58
56
54
52
50
48
46
44
42
40
38
36
34
32
30
28
26
24
22
20
18
16
14
12
10
8
6
4
2
0

1
Date: _____

2
Date: _____

3
Date: _____

4
Date: _____

Observation

Part III

Annotated Bibliography and References

This annotated bibliography is provided for readers who would like to learn more about issues related to supporting teaching and learning from selected research and professional literature. Some studies and articles in this section were briefly introduced in a particular chapter but were not explained in great detail. Other studies and articles in this section were not addressed in the book but offer additional information on best practice in the field related to a specific topic. The annotations are presented in a standard format for ease in referencing and using the information.

Matrix

The matrix that follows is intended as a guide to connect the annotations with key aspects or issues related to supporting teaching and learning. The first column contains the author last names of the reference. The second column provides a link between the annotation and the appropriate chapter. The final column denotes the specific topic addressed in the annotation.

Author	Chapter	Topic
Anderson & Minke (2007)	2	Relationships with parents
Babinski, Jones, & DeWert (2001)	3	Mentoring for first-year teachers
Barbetta, Norona, & Bicard (2005)	4	Classroom management
Borek & Parsons (2004)	4	Time management
Conroy, Sutherland, Snyder, & Marsh (2008)	4	Classroom management
Deslandes & Bertrand (2005)	2	Relationship with parents
Emmer, Evertson, & Worsham (2006)	4	Classroom management
Evertson, Emmer, & Worsham (2006)	4	Classroom management
Fairbanks, Simonsen & Sugai (2008)	4	Classroom management
Hattie (2003)	2	Effective Strategies
Hong & Shull (2009)	2	Dispositions toward students
Klecka, Cheng, & Clift (2004)	3	Mentoring
Lustick & Sykes (2006)	3	Certification and professional development
Matheson & Shriver (2005)	4	Classroom management
Murdock & Miller (2003)	2	Teacher caring
Patrick, Anderman, Ryan, Edelin, & Midgley (2001)	4	Classroom management
Peart & Campbell (1999)	2	Teacher caring
Pogue & AhYun (2006)	2	Motivation
Rogers, Abell, Lannin, Wang, Musikul, Barker, & Dingman (2007)	3	Professional development
Stronge, Ward, Tucker, Hindman, McClosky, & Howard (2008)	3	Certification
Swinson & Harrop (2005)	4	Classroom management
van Duijvenvoorde, Zanolie, Rombouts, Raijmakers, & Crone (2008)	4	Feedback on Behavior
Wallace, 2009	3	Professional Development

Anderson, K. J., & Minke, K. M. (2007). **Parent involvement in education: Toward an understanding of parents' decision making.** *The Journal of Educational Research, 100*(5), 311–323. [Journal article]

The researchers surveyed parents at three low-income (participation in free and reduced-price lunch program ranged from 76% to 98% in the participating schools) urban elementary schools in the same United States school district. Parent response rates at the three schools were 23.8%, 28.9%, and 35.9%, respectively. The Hoover-Dempsey and Sadler Model of Parental Involvement was used to construct a path model to show what influenced parents' decisions to participate in their students' schooling as well as the type of involvement they were engaging in. Parental involvement was considered from the parent's perspective and involves multiple levels. The first level related to *why* parents decide to come involved in their child's education through:

- *Role construction*—What a parent should do because they are the parent.

- *Efficacy*—How parents believe their involvement will influence their child's learning.

The second level relates to *how* the parent becomes involved, which is influenced by the following:

- Parental knowledge that can be shared (e.g., guest speaker, helping with homework);

- Competing demands (e.g., job obligations); and,

- Specific invitations to participate from either the child or the teacher.

Three types of parental involvement were studied: at school events (e.g., concerts), at ongoing school activities (e.g., classroom volunteer), and at home (e.g., homework help). Parents reported larger-than-expected levels of involvement at home, a type of involvement that is less visible to teachers.

The most significant influence on parental involvement both at home and at school was invitation by the teacher. Researchers also found that a parent's sense of efficacy had a significant influence on involvement at home. Role construction and parental knowledge were not significantly influential. In an open-ended question, many parents responded that a caring teacher who communicated valuing parental input also influenced decisions to become involved. For parents with adequate resources, competing demands were not influential; however, for parents with fewer resources, demands were influential in the decision-making process. Regardless, the most significant influence on parental involvement was a specific invitation from the teacher, "when they [parents] perceive that their participation is desired by teachers, they find ways to be involved regardless of their resources" (p. 319).

The researchers noted several other factors that may be influential in parental involvement decisions such as:

- Student invitations to parents to participate;

- Parents' personal experience in school, whether positive or negative; and,

♦ Quality of the parent-teacher relationship—trust is more important than lots of contacts.

Babinski, L. M., Jones, B. D., & DeWert, M. H. (2001). The roles of facilitators and peers in an online support community for first-year teachers. *Journal of Educational and Psychological Consultation, 12(2)*, 151–169. [Journal article]

The Lighthouse Project was an online group mentoring forum for twelve beginning teachers who had all completed their teacher preparation program at the same university. The twelve mentors in the project were comprised of experienced classroom teachers and professors from the teacher preparation program. The mentoring interactions were open to and inclusive of the entire group.

The intent of the program was to provide support and a problem-solving resource to beginning teachers who were teaching in geographically diverse areas. The forum was launched with a day-long, face-to-face orientation and training, in which the participants met and interacted with each other in person prior to interacting with each other in the virtual setting. Initially, communication among the group occurred via an e-mail listserv. Participants posted questions or described concerns, and others responded. During the course of the project, the forum was changed to a Web-based discussion forum using Lotus Notes, but communication remained asynchronous (i.e., not occurring at the same time).

The study of the Lighthouse Project focused on an analysis of frequency of participation and a categorization of topics of discussion. Specifically, the researchers found:

♦ Mentors posted slightly more frequently than novice teachers in the forum.

♦ Novice teachers tended to relate personal experiences in their posts, whereas mentors tended to provide advice or share knowledge.

♦ Approximately 10% of the postings were made up of initiating messages used to prompt discussion.

♦ Eight content categories were evident among the postings. In order of frequency from most to least frequent, the topics of discussion were: (1) individual students, (2) policy and politics, (3) stories about teaching, (4) technical issues, (5) me as a teacher, (6) classroom management, (7) working with adults, and (8) curriculum and instruction.

♦ Five categories were identified as indicating the various purposes of posts to the forum. In order of frequency from most to least frequent, these were: (1) fostering a sense of community, (2) providing advice, (3) sharing knowledge, (4) relating a personal experience with an issue, and (5) encouraging reflection.

Barbetta, P. M., Norona, K. L., & Bicard, D. F. (2005). Classroom behavior management: A dozen common mistakes and what to do instead. *Preventing School Failure, 49*(3), 11–19. [Journal article]

In this resource, twelve common mistakes in behavior management are presented along with suggestions of what could be done differently. The old saying about *an ounce of prevention is worth a pound of cure* is appropriate for this article, which promotes preventing misbehavior or escalation of the situation if misbehavior occurs. The article is summarized in the table below and contains a sample form as well as step-by-step suggestions and examples to promote increased teacher effectiveness with classroom management. Additionally, the article's authors include an appendix of suggested resources organized by "common mistakes" for readers desiring more information.

	Common Mistake*	What to Do Instead
1	Defining behavior by how it looks	*Define misbehavior by its function* Misbehavior is often more a symptom of students trying to get or avoid of something. Addressing misbehavior may temporarily address the symptom, but not the cause. For example, misbehavior may simply be a result of a student's inability to see the overhead. By identifying the student's focus, a teacher can directly address the behavior as opposed to the symptoms.
2	Asking "why did you do that?"	*Assess the behavior directly to determine its function* Gather information about what the student seeks to get from inappropriate actions. Identify what occurred before and as a result of the behavior in order to provide the student with more appropriate alternatives.
3	When an approach isn't working, try harder	*Try another way* Strategies such as praising students, redirection, moving closer to a student, and cueing may provide the desired change in a student's actions when the initial consequence or intervention does not work.
4	Violating the principles of good classroom rules	*Follow the guidelines for classroom rules* Involve students in creating four to six classroom rules that are clear, reasonable, enforceable, generally worded so they can be applied to a variety of classroom interactions, and, ideally, positively stated.
5	Treating all misbehaviors as "won't dos"	*Treat some behaviors as "can't dos"* Consider if students' misbehavior is the result of a lack of skill in handling a situation. Then provide additional opportunities through modeling and practice to develop the skill.

	Common Mistake*	What to Do Instead
6	Lack of planning for transition time	*Appropriately plan for transition time* Develop consistent expectations and routines for transitioning from one activity to another. Explicitly teach students these guidelines and provide feedback.
7	Ignoring all or nothing at all	*Ignore wisely* Combining the practice of ignoring some inappropriate behaviors with behavior-building strategies can be effective as students will learn to use positive behaviors to get their desired intent. Remember that "ignoring teaches students what not to do, but does not teach them what they should do instead" (p. 15).
8	Overuse and misuse of time out	*Follow the principles of effective time out* Create a time-out process whereby the time-out situation is less stimulating than what is occurring in the classroom. During time-out, there is no opportunity for students to be reinforced either positively or negatively.
9	Inconsistent expectations and consequences	*Have clear expectations that are enforced and reinforced consistently* Have students review the expectations for conducting a particular activity prior to starting. Provide feedback to students about how they are meeting expectations.
10	Viewing ourselves as the only classroom manager	*Include students, parents, and others in management efforts* Use others to convey and backup the expectations for those working in the classroom environment. Students can self-monitor their behavior perhaps with a monitoring form or oral cue. Peers can be taught how to reinforce desired behaviors and work to resolve conflicts. Other adults in the building and family members can become apart of effectively conveying and reinforcing desired behaviors.
11	Missing the link between instruction and behavior	*Think of academic instruction as a behavior management tool* Select instructional strategies and effective teaching practices that engage learners.
12	Taking student misbehavior too personally	*Take student misbehavior professionally, not personally* Anticipate common behavioral issues and plan for how to prevent them. Develop a management plan, so that if misbehavior occurs, the response is already thought out. Finally, recognize that some behaviors take a lot more time and effort to change and invest in that change.

*The wording of the "Common Mistake" and the italicized portions under "What to Do Instead" are direct quotes from the article.

Borek, J., & Parsons, S. (2004). Research on improving teacher time management. *Academic Exchange Quarterly, 8*(3), 27–30. [Journal article]

Shelly Parsons (coauthor of the article) is an elementary school teacher who wanted to improve her time-management skills. She recognized that time was a factor in her professional practice. Additionally, the authors noted that "teacher's time expenditure is also influenced by the increasing needs of students" (p. 27). She had two students with attention deficit hyperactivity disorder (ADHD) in her classroom.

She used a couple of strategies suggested in *Teacher's Time Management Survival Kit: Ready to Use Techniques and Materials*—homework and make-up work strategies—with her third graders. She recorded how the use of the strategies affected her time. Below are summaries of the strategies.

♦ *Homework Strategy* entailed arranging students' desks into groups. For each group a student was assigned to serve as a homework monitor. This student used a form to record who had homework to turn in and who did not. Then he attached the form to the top of the completed papers and gave them to the teacher. In the event that a student did not have his/her homework, the monitor asked the student fill out a "homework excuse form," which was also given to the teacher.

♦ *Make-Up Work Strategy* involved using a "homework/make-up agreement form" that the teacher filled out and discussed with students. The form included consequences for failure to turn in homework as well as due date. This form was attached to students' work. Then as assignments were returned, the teacher checked off on the form what was submitted.

The teacher reported that prior to implementing the strategies, she routinely left school around 6 P.M. each day; however, after she started using these strategies, she was able to leave by 4 P.M. The following table (page 106) explains the benefits of these strategies.

Strategy	Implementation		Benefits
	Before	**After**	
Homework	Seven to ten minutes per subject spent each day on collecting homework	Same amount of time	◆ Increased student ownership of the process ◆ Reduced interruptions by students as they had a forum to explain why they were missing homework (homework excuse form) ◆ Increased homework submissions as excuse forms were copied and sent home ◆ Increased in class time the teacher had to respond to parental notes or grade papers
Make-Up Work	Teacher experienced frustration with remembering to give the work and requesting to get the work back	Time was saved	◆ Increased organization of the make-up work procedure from documenting assignments to students submitting work with the contract stapled on top ◆ Increased students' sense of responsibility and the importance of submitting completed make-up work as students signed contracts with the teacher ◆ Provided a source of documentation ◆ Reduced followup time that previously was used to ask students about their make-up work

Conroy, M. A., Sutherland, K. S., Snyder, A. L., & Marsh, S. (2008). Classwide interventions: Effective instruction makes a difference. *Teaching Exceptional Children, 40*(6), 24–30. [Journal article]

The authors of this article offer a list of research-based, classwide intervention strategies to use in both preventing and responding to behavior in the classroom. Classwide intervention strategies are those that combine more than one best practice in managing the classroom. They explain that these strategies are aimed at two different approaches: to manipulate the environment in order to increase positive behavior and to manipulate the consequences, which may be either positive or negative. Six strategies that lead to positive classroom climates include (the verbatim names of the strategies are used):

◆ *Close Supervision and Monitoring*—This strategy includes being around the students and actively engaged with them. Another term used in educational circles is *proximity*. Proximity can be used to prevent disruptions from occurring in the first place and to intervene quickly when a problem arises. A useful tool in monitoring includes zone monitoring in which a teacher with the assistance of a paraprofessional monitors specific zones in the classroom.

♦ *Classroom Rules*—Just as a teacher provides academic expectations, a teacher must also provide behavioral expectations. These expectations are communicated to students, and in some cases developed along with students, are set at the beginning of the year, and are explicitly taught to students. Student behavior is monitored and both positive and negative consequences are applied.

♦ *Opportunities to Respond*—The authors connect behavior and academics in that using questioning and prompting to engage learners means that they are involved in the lesson. Engagement then leads to a more positive classroom environment. According to studies cited by the authors, when prompting and questioning are increased so is on-task behavior.

♦ *Contingent Praise*—Positive praise is a way to reinforce desired behaviors. The authors share that effective praise is both specific and contingent. Specific praise lets the child know exactly what behavior the child exhibited that is desired. Contingent praise means that praise is given when a desired behavior occurs. Positive praise is more desired than corrective statements and that teachers should provide more positive praise than correction.

♦ *Feedback, Error Correction, and Progress Monitoring*—Feedback in academic work and providing specific information regarding error correction are associated with increased engagement and a more positive classroom environment.

♦ *Good Behavior Game (GBG)*—This strategy is a specific tool that is likened to cooperative learning in which students assess their peers in behavior. Students are assigned to teams and if a student on the team violates a classroom rule, the team receives a check by the team name. At the end of the instructional session, the team or teams that meet the criteria for winning receive a reward.

The authors conclude that a combination of these research-based strategies typically will be used to maximize effectiveness.

Deslandes, R., & Bertrand, R. (2005). Motivation of parent involvement in secondary-level schooling. *The Journal of Educational Research, 98*(3), 164–175. [Journal article]

The researchers surveyed 770 parents of adolescents in five schools in Quebec (51% response rate). A variety of respondent variables were controlled for, such as gender, family structure, and education level. The Hoover-Dempsey and Sadler Model of Parental Involvement (described in the Anderson & Minke annotation) was used to explain the variance in why parents decided to participate in students' schooling.

Specific invitations by students and specific invitations from teachers were consistent across the grade levels as reasons why parents chose to become involved. Parents were likely to become involved if their student specifically asked them for help such as reviewing work, generating report ideas, or observing a skill. Interestingly, parents were likely to respond to teachers' invitations for school involvement, but not for involvement at home. The researchers attributed the parental inclination to let students invite them to become involved as an indication that parents are recognizing increasing adolescent autonomy. Neither parental knowledge nor competing demands significantly accounted for the variance in parental involvement decisions. Parental efficacy was influential at home in grades 7 and 8, but not in grade 9.

Role construction (e.g., how parents perceived their duty as parents) explained some of the variance in grades 7 and 9. That is, parents of seventh graders reported involvement at school and home as part of their responsibility as parents, whereas parents of ninth graders reported doing their duty as it occurred in the school setting, such as parent–teacher conferences. The researchers recommend the following steps to increase parental involvement:

- ◆ At home…
  - ◆ Let students know the value of asking parents to be involved.
  - ◆ Coach students on how to involve a family member.
  - ◆ Share with parents the benefits of their involvement at home.
- ◆ At school…
  - ◆ Initiate individual contacts.
  - ◆ Develop trusting parent–teacher relationships.

Emmer, E. T., Evertson, C. M., & Worsham, M. E. (2006). *Classroom management for middle and high school teachers* **(7th ed.). Boston, MA: Allyn and Bacon. [Book]**

Evertson, C. M., Emmer, E. T., & Worsham, M. E. (2006). *Classroom management for elementary teachers* **(7th ed.). Boston, MA: Allyn and Bacon. [Book]**

These two resources are listed and annotated together as the authors provide the research behind and best practices in classroom management for both elementary teachers and secondary teachers. The authors demonstrate clearly the connection between good, effective instruction and a positive learning environment. The chapters address the following aspects related to classroom management:

- ◆ Chapters 1 and 2 discuss the research related to classroom organization as well as the establishment of classroom rules and efficient routines and procedures.
- ◆ Chapters 3 and 4 focus on the importance of prior planning in deciding on how to keep student records and how best to provide feedback to students

as well as the importance of establishing a positive environment on the first and second day of school through careful planning of activities.

- ◆ Chapters 7 and 9 involve responding to student behavior and dealing with problem behaviors.

- ◆ Chapters 6 and 10 focus on the importance of managing groups, such as co-operative learning groups, working within a heterogeneous classroom, and helping students with special needs.

- ◆ Chapter 8 examines the importance of communication for the effective teacher. A teacher who is able to communicate both content and classroom directions clearly will be more effective in both classroom instruction and in managing the classroom.

Each book provides specific ideas related to the content and the school level of the student. The chapters provide practical applications and readers are encouraged to use a checklist at the end of each chapter to ensure that they have attended to important aspects related to classroom management in their own practice.

Fairbanks, S., Simonsen, B., & Sugai, G. (2008). Classwide secondary and tertiary tier practices and systems. *Teaching Exceptional Children* 40(6), 44–52. [Journal article]

The authors of this article offer a three-tier approach to intervention in the classroom. The first, or primary tier, includes classwide management practices. These include establishing classroom rules, monitoring and responding to student behavior, and engaging students through questioning and prompting. However, the authors acknowledge that some students do not respond to primary interventions and may need additional intervention. This is called the secondary tier.

Key features of secondary tier interventions include targeting specific skills and providing instruction on those skills, teaching students how to monitor their own behavior, acknowledging when students exhibit positive behaviors, providing regular feedback on target skills, and using peers in the classroom to help other students. One specific example of a secondary tier intervention the authors provide is called "Check In, Check Out" (CICO). In CICO, the teacher checks in with the student at the beginning of the day to review targeted behaviors, monitors student behavior at regular intervals, and provides a rating for student behavior. Students receive a certain number of points for the ratings which are tallied at the end of the day, which is "check out."

Some students may not respond to secondary tier interventions and may require an additional level of support, the tertiary tier. Tertiary tier intervention involves the creation of an individualized behavior plan. This plan is developed by educational professionals and family representatives including the teacher, parents or guardians, and other specialists, for example, a behavior specialist. Tertiary interventions include assistance to the teacher, teaching the student to monitor his or her own behavior as well as social skills, reducing the length of time students are engaged in a task by dividing the task into smaller increments, working with other adults and taking breaks during the day, and allowing for student-preferred activities.

The authors worked with four teachers with twelve total students in two schools to implement the three-tiered approach to intervention. The authors described that most wanted to move directly to secondary and tertiary tier intervention but began with primary intervention. After primary interventions were in place and used with students, four of the twelve students did not respond and required further intervention. After secondary tier intervention was implemented, two students responded positively and two required tertiary tier interventions. Following tertiary tier interventions, the problem behaviors for these two students was reduced. Before the researchers worked with the four teachers, the teachers thought that most children would require at least secondary interventions. The teachers believed that the students would need more intervention than was actually necessary. The researchers argue that with a defined intervention plan, most behaviors can be addressed in the primary tier and more severe interventions will not be necessary.

Hattie, J. (2003, October). *Teachers make a difference: What is the research evidence?* **Background paper to invited address presented at the 2003 ACER Research Conference, Melbourne, Australia. Retrieved from www.acer.edu. au [Conference proceeding]**

John Hattie reviewed more than 500,000 studies and found that differences in student outcomes could be attributed to teachers 30% of the time. School, peers, and home-related factors accounted for 20% of the variance, and the remaining 50% were related to the individual student. He wrote that "it is what teachers know, do, and care about that is very powerful in the learning equation" (p. 2). He found a number of teacher-related influences on learning that appear in the Top 10 list below. The numbers in parentheses are the effect sizes, which are a measurement of how much impact a particular item has when comparing different groups; the numbers range from a low of 0 for no impact to a high of 2. The quality of instruction was second only to the feedback that teachers give students on influencing student achievement.

> **Top 10 Influences on Student Outcomes**
>
> 1. Feedback (1.13)
> 2. Instructional quality (1)
> 3. Direct instruction (0.82)
> 4. Remediation/feedback (0.65)
> 5. Class environment (0.56)
> 6. Challenge of goals (0.5)
> 7. Mastery learning (0.5)
> 8. Homework (0.43)
> 9. Teacher style (0.42)
> 10. Questioning (0.41)

Hong, B., & Shull, P. (2009, April). Impact of Teacher Dispositions on Student Self-determination. *International Journal of Learning, 16*(1), 261–271. [Journal article]

Students want to be treated as people, not widgets. When teachers show an interest in their students, the students' sense of self-belief and self-worth is often increased. Caring was a predominate theme found throughout the data in the study.

The study found that teacher dispositions could predict their students' sense of self-determination. All four of the following teacher dispositions were statistically significant with teacher quality being the best predictor followed by student treatment. Each of the following dispositions refers to the words and actions a teacher does.

- ◆ Relatedness focuses on the attachment bond between student and teacher.

- ◆ Responsiveness refers to how the teacher demonstrates caring, empathy, patience, and in general, interest in the overall well-being of the student.

- ◆ Student treatment is how the teacher respects and acts toward the individual student.

- ◆ Teacher quality are the nuts and bolts of the teacher being effective in promoting the student's learning.

Fifty-nine East Coast, suburban, high school students completed two instruments, the Student Perception of Teacher Dispositions Scale and the Arc's Self-Determination Scale. The self determination scale had four subscales: autonomy, psychological empowerment, self-realization, and self-regulation.

The study was a mixed design consisting of the survey data and case studies, which contributed depth to the findings in the survey. The three students interviewed indicated that they wanted timely feedback, engaging lessons, opportunity to make decisions, access to teachers when help was needed, and to be treated as an individual as opposed to a "nobody."

Most students strongly agreed (56%) or agreed (29%) that their teachers were responsive to them. Overall, students strongly agreed (44%) or agreed (34%) that teachers demonstrated positive dispositions toward them. Relatedness (19%) and teacher quality (10%) had the largest percentages of students disagreeing on how teachers acted toward them. On the open-ended survey question items, "the most cited manners of teachers can be summed up as follow: listen, help, talk, encourage, be fair, take more time, do not force, give choices, believe, respect, understand, give feedback, be available, accept, and care about me" (p. 269).

Klecka, C. L, Cheng, Y., & Clift, R. T. (2004). Exploring the potential of electronic mentoring. *Action in Teacher Education, 26*(3), 2–9. [Journal article]

This study describes the Novice Teacher Support Project (NTSP) located in Illinois, which (at the time of the study) was comprised of a university, two regional offices, and more than twenty school districts. The forum was an "e-conferencing environment consisting of threaded conversations" (p. 3), designed to prompt and facilitate professional conversations among prekindergarten through twelfth grade beginning and experienced teachers. During the three years reported, the number of participants was 115, 138, and 82, respectively. The forum was password-protected, and neither school nor district administrators had access to the forum.

Using a mixed-methods design, the researchers made several findings and drew tentative conclusions about the e-conferencing format of online mentoring, including the following:

♦ Organizers play a critically important role in facilitating communication, focusing on practical, relevant topics, and ensuring an environment that is respectful of all participants.

♦ Compensation may provide an incentive for teachers to overcome perceived barriers to participation in an online forum, such as hesitancy to share concerns with others, time constraints, and lack of comfort with a computer-based environment.

♦ Structured training in the use of the technology used for the forum and ongoing support are necessary to facilitate the virtual community.

♦ Many new teachers do not want to be perceived as "begging for advice" (p. 8).

♦ Novice teachers appreciated the anonymity of online mentoring.

♦ Novice teachers posted less frequently than mentor teachers. Yet, novice teachers read the posts, a legitimate means of benefiting from the discussion forum.

♦ Novice and mentor teachers alike reported that the e-conferencing prompted professional and personal relationships that may not have formed otherwise.

Lustick, D., & Sykes, G. (2006). National board certification as professional development: What are teachers learning? *Education Policy Analysis Archives, 14*(5). Retrieved from http://epaa.asu.edu/epaa/v14n5/ [Journal article]

Researchers in this study were interested in determining the effects of the National Board for Professional Teaching Standards (NBPTS) certification process on the professional development of teachers. The study followed 120 candidates for the Adolescent and Young Adult Science Certificate for two years. Using structured interviews and assessment rubrics, the researchers examined what teachers learn by participating in the National Board Certification (NBC) process. Some teachers reported that the process enhanced their current understandings, whereas others reported that they had to change some of their practices. The NBC process served as professional development for teachers as they critically examined their professional practices and grew professionally. In particular scientific inquiry and assessment-related standards had the greatest gains. These gains were observed regardless of whether the teacher was successful in obtaining NBC. One teacher shared that her practice was "enriched by assessment, as it becomes a tool for improving student learning instead of a requirement at unit's end" (p. 24). Going through the process of NBC had an overall effect of 0.47 on candidates understanding of knowledge associated with science teaching when examining collected pre- and post-NBC evidence.

> Effect sizes range from a low of 0, for no impact, to a high of 2. So an overall effect of 0.47 is noteworthy.

In examining the interviews the researchers identified three types of learning through the NBPTS certification process:

- *Dynamic*—This type of learning is defined as immediate change in a teacher's knowledge, skills, and/or attitudes in teaching science.

- *Technical*—Although they were learning how to achieve certification, these new understandings did not necessarily translate into their work as teachers.

- *Deferred*—After the certification process, teachers had time to reflect on the process itself and the new understandings they had gained. The teachers reflected on what they learned and how they might be able to use this new knowledge at some future time.

Of the 13 NBPTS standards, the researchers found significant differences between teachers' abilities in scientific inquiry and assessment before and after the certification process. In the interviews, participants commented most on scientific inquiry, assessment, and interpreting learning outcomes.

The researchers concluded that:

- The NBPTS certification process is a worthwhile professional development activity for teachers, as teacher abilities in two standard areas changed in a positive direction, and

- Teachers should receive financial assistance to pursue NBPTS certification, and or, receive some financial incentive for obtaining certification.

NBPTS *Standards for Accomplished Teaching in AYA Science* at the time of the study appear below.

♦ Preparing the Way for Productive Student Learning
  • Understanding Students
  • Knowledge of Science
  • Instructional Resources
♦ Advancing Student Learning
  • Science Inquiry
  • Conceptual Understandings
  • Contexts of Science
♦ Establishing a Favorable Context for Learning
  • Engagement
  • Equitable Participation
  • Learning Environment
♦ Supporting Teaching and Student Learning
  • Family and Community Outreach
  • Assessment
  • Reflection
  • Collegiality and Leadership

Matheson, A. S., & Shriver, M. D. (2005). Training teachers to give effective commands: Effects on student compliance and academic behaviors. *School Psychology Review, 34*(2), 202–219. [Journal article]

The teachers of three disruptive lower-elementary students were nominated by their principal to participate in a study on giving effective commands. During observations, researchers found that the three students complied with their teachers' requests less than half the time that their peers did. The researchers reasoned that students' success in school was predicated on their compliance with teacher directions and instruction. They divided school tasks into two types of behavior:

♦ *Academic engagement*—the time in which students are participating in instruction, and

♦ *Academic responding*—when students are doing what is asked of them, such as reading silently, writing, answering questions.

Prior research in the area of effective parental command use had "identified effective commands as those that are directly stated, are specific and consist of one step, are developmentally appropriate, are phrased positively, and are given one at a time (e.g., there is at least a 5-second wait time between commands)" (p. 203). The research literature also indicated that when parents received training in giving effective commands, children were more apt to comply.

The researchers applied the results of studies of parental commands to teaching. The three students' teachers participated in two training sessions on giving effective commands (a) using a quiet voice tone, (b) stating the command in precise and concise language, and (c) being specific about the desired outcome. The teachers also were trained to distinguish between alpha and beta commands. Alpha commands typically consist of one verb, such as "Quietly *start* reading at page 97 in your social studies book." Beta commands have more than one verb such as, "*Take* out your social studies book, *turn* to page 97, and quietly *start* reading." Furthermore, the teachers received training in giving positive praise when students complied. The study was conducted in three phases:

♦ Phase 1—baseline information (what was typical before training);

♦ Phase 2—impact of effective command giving training; and,

♦ Phase 3—impact of effective commands and praise giving training.

Findings showed that all teachers improved in their ability to give effective commands. Their students' compliance also increased. Initially, teachers phrased commands effectively 46% to 57% of the time. The students whose responses were being observed complied 22% to 50% of the time. With training, the teachers increased effective command usage to 81% to 87%, and at the same time their students' rates of compliance increased to 57% to 71%. Upon receiving training using praise with effective commands, teachers' percentages ranged from a slight decrease of 79% to an increase of 93%. Similarly, the students' numbers increased to a compliance high of 66% to 84%. In summary, training made a difference. When students knew what was expected of them, they were able to perform.

Murdock, T. B., & Miller, A. (2003). Teachers as sources of middle school students' motivational identity: Variable-centered and person-centered analytic approaches. *The Elementary School Journal, 103*(4), 383–399. [Journal article]

A study examined the perceptions of 206 eighth grade students to determine the relationship between the students' achievement and their perception that their teacher cared. The students ethnicity of the group was 50% white and 44% African American. Forty-five percent of the students in the study participated in the free or reduced price lunch program.

Teacher caring was defined in the study as "including interpersonal support and respect, as well as behaviors that demonstrate a commitment to student learning, such as setting high expectations and coming to class prepared to teach" (p. 385). Teachers rated students' effort in core subjects, and students completed three instruments that measured academic self-efficacy, intrinsic valuing of education, and parental attachment. Findings showed that teacher caring significantly affected student motivation.

Motivation is a complex and interrelated outcome that is influenced by multiple factors. For example, when examining perceptions of teacher caring and academic self-efficacy, the difference is 21%. However, motivational influences include parents, peers, and students' prior motivation in addition to the teacher's caring. When the other influences are statistically removed (i.e., accounted/controlled for) the impact of teacher caring is 5%. Over time, this 5% has a cumulative long-term effect such that caring teacher has affected students in a positive way that continues even after the student leaves the teacher's classroom.

Patrick, H., Anderman, L. H., Ryan, A. M., Edelin, K. C., & Midgley, C. (2001). Teachers' communication of goal orientations in four fifth grade classrooms. *The Elementary School Journal, 102*(1), 35–58. [Journal article]

Using surveys and observations, researchers studied 223 fifth grade students in ten classrooms to identify different levels of motivation and performance, specifically how teachers explicitly and implicitly communicated mastery and performance goals to their students. The classrooms were observed multiple times (990 minutes per class) during the first three weeks of school, including the first day of class, and later during the school year (three ninety-minute observations in one week).

The data from two high-mastery and two low-mastery classrooms were selected for further analysis. The teachers in the two high-mastery classrooms had four and eleven years of teaching experience, respectively, whereas the teachers in the low-mastery classrooms had twenty-four and twenty-six years of teaching experience, respectively. The high-mastery classes had twenty-nine and twenty-four students, respectively, whereas the low-mastery classrooms had thirty students each.

The following table shows the differences identified between the two classrooms in eight areas.

Focus	Teacher Talk Teacher Practices	
	High-Mastery Classroom	**Low-Mastery Classroom**
Task (i.e., content, classroom procedures, participation, affect, task message)	♦ Ensured equitable student participation ♦ Communicated enthusiasm and care for students ♦ A teacher said, "There are three ways to learn: from seeing, hearing, and doing. I will try to use all of those ways" (p. 45)	♦ One teacher indicated that she called on nonvolunteers as "punishment for not paying attention" (p. 43) ♦ Conveyed little interest in students ♦ A teacher said, "most learning takes place when we learn to listen" (p. 45)
	Both groups experienced similar types of assignments and procedures, but the outcomes were different.	
	Emphasized understanding and improvement	Emphasized getting the right answer

Focus	Teacher Talk Teacher Practices	
	High-Mastery Classroom	**Low-Mastery Classroom**
Authority within the classroom (i.e., rules, autonomy)	♦ Discussed rules and role models ♦ Used praise for making good choices	One teacher spoke for three hours on the first day of school on the importance of listening to the teacher and following rules
	Students had the freedom to make choices as long as they remained focused on academics	Emphasized sanctions and importance of following directions
Recognition of student interest/ability	"Yesterday I told him not to put 'I saw a slug and a spider and a grasshopper and a beetle,' and he paid attention" (p. 47)—teacher reading from a student's work and praising comma usage	A teacher said, "You both have those items out...and are now sitting quietly" (p. 47)
	Clear, academically focused, and targeted feedback for individuals as well as the class	♦ Verbal recognition was related to behavior ♦ No verbal confidence in students' abilities was conveyed
Grouping of students for instructional purposes	No clear pattern between the two classroom groups. Much of the instruction observed was either whole-class or individual.	
Evaluation of student progress and communication of purpose of evaluation	A teacher said, "Even though you are showing mistakes in your portfolio, that's okay because it's showing learning" (p. 50)	A teacher said, "Last year the top two people in this class were the top two girls in the district" (p. 49)
	Tests were presented as a matter of course—without judgment	Emphasized the importance of testing and grades for prestige and demonstration of ability
Time—Use of instructional time	No clear pattern between the two classroom groups; however, variations occurred by teacher within the two groups	

Focus	Teacher Talk Teacher Practices	
	High-Mastery Classroom	Low-Mastery Classroom
♦ Social (i.e., student inter- action, teacher–student interaction) ♦ Classroom interactions among students and teacher	No clear pattern between the two classroom groups; how- ever, variations occurred by teacher within the two groups	
Help-seeking	No clear pattern between the two classroom groups; how- ever, variations occurred by teacher within the two groups	

Peart, N. A., & Campbell, F. A. (1999). At-risk students' perceptions of teacher effectiveness. *Journal for a Just and Caring Education, 5*(3), 269–284. [Journal article]

Forty-seven African American adults were asked what characteristics of effective teachers made a difference for them. Not surprisingly, they shared that racial impartiality was important. Their best teachers treated students equitably. They also recalled effective teachers as those who had good interpersonal, communication, and motivation skills. The following table provides examples of the type of skill and positive examples related to that skill.

Type of Skill	Positive Examples
Interpersonal	♦ Showed interest in the student as an individual ♦ Demonstrated caring, concern, and empathy toward student ♦ Demonstrated appropriate teacher self-disclosure ♦ Was accessible ♦ Established a positive student-teacher relationship
Communication	♦ Demonstrated command of the content ♦ Displayed enthusiasm for the subject matter ♦ Effectively taught the material
Motivation	♦ Set high expectations for academic success ♦ Encouraged students to take responsibility for learning ♦ Challenged learners appropriately ♦ Offered reinforcement and encouragement

Pogue, L. L., & AhYun, K. (2006). The effect of teacher nonverbal immediacy and credibility on student motivation and affective learning. *Communication Education, 55*(3), 331–345. [Journal article]

This study addressed the issue of what students perceive as more important—credibility or immediacy. Nonverbal immediacy (e.g., eye contact, facial expression, friendly, distant) was contrasted with teacher credibility (e.g., content knowledge, feedback, student treatment). The participants, 586 college students, read one of four scenarios and were instructed to imagine taking a class from the teacher described in the scenario. Then they completed questionnaires related to motivation and affective learning.

Average for Motivation and Affective Learning by Scenario

	Low Immediacy (e.g., reserved, tense, aloof)	High Immediacy (e.g., smile, approachable, eye contact)
Low Credibility (e.g., uneven treatment of students, weak feedback, unsure of content)	Motivation = 2.47 Affective Learning = 2.58	Motivation = 3.51 Affective Learning = 3.47
High Credibility (e.g., answers questions well, follows through)	Motivation = 3.50 Affective Learning = 4.10	Motivation = 5.75 Affective Learning = 6.16

Results showed that high credibility and high immediacy had the strongest effect on both motivation and affective learning. Furthermore, for motivation, the ratings given on the low/low and high/high (shaded portions) were statistically significant from the low/high groups. For affective learning, all the means were statistically significant. The researchers concluded that immediacy and credibility both affect motivation, but neither is more important than the other. However, immediacy is a means to increase affective outcomes.

Rogers, M. P., Abell, S., Lannin, J., Wang, C., Musikul, K., Barker, D., & Dingman, S. (2007). Effective professional development in science and mathematics education: Teachers' and facilitators' views. *International Journal of Science and Mathematics Education, 5,* 507–532. [Journal article]

Seventy-two teachers and twenty-three professional development facilitators participated in semistructured interviews that were analyzed to determine what each group thought constituted effective professional development. The participants all participated in two- to three-week long professional development summer institutes that emphasized inquiry and hands-on experiences. They represented 143 schools in seventy-six school districts in one state. Their responses were compared to each other as well as the research base on professional development from researchers. Both groups expressed a value for similar attributes of professional development, but with different interpretations of the attribute (see table below). The authors of the study noted that the research base suggested that there were three aspects of effective professional development that neither group identified: challenging teachers' beliefs and subject-matter knowledge, encouraging teachers to apply learning from the professional development to their schools in a leadership role, and using student learning as a means to gauge the effectiveness of the professional development. As facilitators seek to make professional development more worthwhile, they need to work to align the reality of what people seek and experience with the ideal of what research suggests works.

Attribute	Elaboration on the Desired Attributes of Effective Professional Development	
	Teachers	Facilitators
Classroom Application	Provision of resources (e.g., equipment, handouts) and activities requiring little modification for implementation, as well as meeting grade-specific curricular needs, in particular areas that teachers' perceived as weaknesses in their instruction. Of the four attributes highlighted, only this attributed was discussed in a similar manner between the two groups. Teachers mentioned this attribute most frequently.	
Teacher as Learner	Experiences that let teachers experience the concepts and learning like their students would. This allowed them to think through how the activity or strategy would work in their classrooms both in terms of pros and challenges. Teachers then could transfer the experiences back to their classrooms.	Learning occurs in three ways: 1. Modeling research-based practices 2. Letting teachers experience the activity as their students would (same as teachers) 3. Providing time for discussion and reflection
Support	Networking activities between teachers, such as engagement in activities with fellow teachers related to the professional development activity to build a colleague-based support system, were described by this group. The networking may be formal (required and structured) or informal (during free time during the professional development or through e-mail during the school year).	Collegiality between teachers and this group is a focus for facilitators who would like to begin to build trusting and supportive relationships with teachers. Facilitators need to listen to teachers to address teachers' needs.

Teacher Content Knowledge		Improvement of teachers' content knowledge so that teachers can help students understand the material. This is done by broadening content knowledge, understanding the content behind an activity, and thinking at a higher level about the content. Facilitators mentioned this attribute most frequently.

Stronge, J. H., Ward, T. J., Tucker, P. D., Hindman, J. L., McClosky, W., & Howard, B. (2008). National board certified teachers and non-national board certified teachers: Is there a difference in teacher effectiveness and student achievement? *Journal of Personnel Evaluation in Education, 20*(3–4), 185–210. [Journal article]

Researchers conducted a two-phase study consisting of an analysis of student achievement data and classroom observation. In Phase I, reading and mathematics student test scores linked to 307 fifth grade North Carolina teachers in three school districts were used to calculate teacher effectiveness indices. Twenty-five of these teachers were National Board Certified Teachers (NBCTs). Using statistical processes (hierarchical linear modeling and least squares ordinary) researchers controlled for student and school demographic influences.

Based on the teacher effectiveness indices that were developed, all teachers were divided into quartiles, Analyses showed that 47% of the Board-certified teachers were in the upper quartiles for mathematics and 61% were in the upper quartiles for reading. Interestingly, 20% of the Board-certified teachers fell in the lowest quartile.

Teachers whose teacher effectiveness indices were in the highest and lowest quartiles for gain scores were invited to participate in Phase II of the study. All teachers submitted a sample of typical assignments, completed a teacher efficacy survey, participated in an interview on planning and assessment practices, and were observed in their classrooms. The observers recorded data related to classroom events, levels of questions asked, and student time-on-task. Additionally, observers completed a teacher effectiveness rating scale. Results showed that Board-certified teachers scored higher than non–Board-certified teachers for clarity of grading criteria, cognitive challenge of assignments, and planning practices. However, NBCT and non–Board-certified upper-quartile teachers were virtually indistinguishable on in-classroom measures.

Swinson, J., & Harrop, A. (2005). An examination of the effects of a short course aimed at enabling teachers in infant, junior and secondary schools to alter the verbal feedback given to their pupils. *Educational Studies, 31*(2), 115–130. [Journal article]

Two British researchers conducted a study of nineteen teachers who were trained to use positive praise to acknowledge good behavior. The training focused first providing feedback to teachers on the negative versus positive feedback provided to students during a pre-training lesson. Teachers were trained in how to use "Four Essential Steps." These essential steps were:

1. Have clear expectations;

2. Seek the desired behavior;

3. Acknowledge students frequently for doing what is right; and,

4. Alter the pace of the authentic feedback.

After the training, the researchers found that teachers reprimanded students less after the training, dropping from 54% of the time to 15% of the time. A purpose of the training was to reduce the negative feedback or disapproval students received from teachers. This goal was achieved in terms of the reduction of negative feedback. A second goal was to increase students' on-task behavior. The researchers found that on average 94% of students were obeying their teachers. The study mirrors results the researchers found with students with behavioral disabilities.

van Duijvenvoorde, A. C. K., Zanolie, K., Rombouts, S. A. R. B., Raijmakers, M. E. J., & Crone, E. A. (2008). Evaluating the negative or valuing the positive? Neural mechanisms supporting feedback-based learning across development. *The Journal of Neuroscience, 28*(38), 9495–9503. [Journal article]

A study of Dutch children (eight- and nine-year-olds), adolescents (eleven- to thirteen-year-olds), and young adults (eighteen- to twenty-five-year-olds) investigated the neural developmental changes as they applied to the use of positive or negative feedback. Fifty-five participants, all with similar intelligence scores, had their brain activity monitored with magnetic resonance imaging (MRI) while they completed a task. The study found that children responded more to positive feedback and young adults to negative feedback when examining (a) after feedback behavior and (b) brain activity. Adolescents did not show a significant preference for either positive or negative feedback. Furthermore, young adults significantly improved than the other two groups when they received feedback on the task. The young adults also had faster response times than the other two groups. When children received negative feedback, their performance accuracy decreased. In examining the MRI for the eight- and nine-year-old group, there was no significant activation of the brain, suggesting that this age group had more difficulty interpreting and acting upon the negative feedback. Overall, performance, accuracy, and response time went up as the participants' age groups increased.

Wallace, M. R. (2009). Making sense of the links: Professional development, teacher practices, and student achievement. *Teachers College Record, 111*(2), 573–596.

Analysis of six databases (i.e., 2000 Beginning Teacher Preparation Survey in Connecticut and Tennessee; National Assessment of Educational Progress [NAEP] in 1996; 2000 in Mathematics; NAEP in 1998; 2000 in Reading) found some relationship among professional development, teacher practices (e.g., what occurs in the classroom), and student achievement. The researcher created a statistical model that controlled for teacher characteristics (e.g., subject-matter knowledge, efficacy) and preparation program in order to examine the effect of professional development on (a) teaching and (b) student achievement as measured by standardized tests. She found that professional development did influence what occurred in the classroom and in some datasets significantly related to student achievement. The study initially focused on professional development, yet the analysis of teacher practices found that they were more influential on student achievement than professional development. More noteworthy is that most of the difference (68% to 85% in mathematics and 50% to 75% in reading [the ranges reflect the different findings from the databases used]) could not be explained by the model which considered professional development and teacher practices. The author writes that the variance may be related to factors such as, "teachers' personal backgrounds, individual styles, peer influences, school climates…that clearly appear to have great influence on the frequency of practices that teachers use" (p. 589).

References

Abbott, L. (2003). Novice teachers' experiences with telementoring as learner-centered professional development. *Dissertation Abstracts Online, 568.* (AA 13116246)

Adams, J.E. (2000). *Taking charge of curriculum: Teacher networks and curriculum implementation.* New York, NY: Teachers College Press.

Adams, C.R. & Singh, K. (1998). Direct and indirect effects of school learning variables on the academic achievement of African American 10th graders. *The Journal of Negro Education, 67*(1), 48–66.

Agne, K.J. (1992). Caring: The expert teacher's edge. *Educational Horizons,* 120–124.

Allday, R. A., & Pakurar, K. (2007). Effect of teacher greetings on student on-task behavior. *Journal of Applied Behavior Analysis, 40*(2), 317–320.

Allen, M., Witt, P. L., & Wheeless, L. R. (2006). The role of teacher immediacy as a motivational factor in student learning: using meta-analysis to test a causal model. *Communication Education, 55*(1), 21–31. Retrieved from http://find.galegroup.com.proxy.wm.edu/itx/start.do?prodId=EAIM

Allington, R. (2002). What I've learned about effective reading instruction. *Phi Delta Kappan, 83*(10), 740–747.

Alvarado, A. (2006*). New directions in teacher education: Emerging strategies from the Teachers for a New Era initiative.* A paper presented at the American Educational Research Association, San Francisco, CA.

Anderson, T. (2005). Why teach? *Kappa Delta Pi Record, 41*(3), 144.

Anderson, K. J., & Minke, K. M. (2007). Parent involvement in education: Toward an understanding of parents' decision making. *The Journal of Educational Research, 100*(5), 311–323.

Babinski, L. M., Jones, B. D., & DeWert, M. H. (2001). The roles of facilitators and peers in an online support community for first-year teachers. *Journal of Educational and Psychological Consultation, 12*(2), 151–169.

Bain, H.P., & Jacobs, R. (1990). The case for smaller classes and better teachers. [Booklet.] *Streamlined seminar—National Association of Elementary School Principals, 9*(1).

Baker, J.A. (1999). Teacher-student interaction in urban at-risk classrooms: Differential behavior, relationship quality, and student satisfaction. *The Elementary School Journal, 100*(1), 57–70.

Barbetta, P. M., Norona, K. L., & Bicard, D. F. (2005). Classroom behavior management: A dozen common mistakes and what to do instead. *Preventing School Failure, 49*(3), 11–19.

Baum, A. C., & McMurray-Schwarz, P. (2004). Preservice teachers' beliefs about family involvement: Implications for teacher education. *Early Childhood Education, 32*(1), 57–162.

Berliner, D. C. (1986). In pursuit of the expert pedagogue. *Educational Researcher, 15*(7), 5–13.

Bernard, B. (2003). Turnaround teachers and schools. In B. Williams (Ed.), *Closing the achievement gap: A vision for changing beliefs and practices* (pp. 115–137). Alexandria, VA: Association for Supervision and Curriculum Development.

Black, L. (2004). Teacher-pupil talk in whole-class discussions and processes of social positioning within the primary school classroom. *Language and Education, 18*(5), 347–360.

Borek, J., & Parsons, S. (2004). Research on improving teacher time management. *Academic Exchange Quarterly 8*(3), 27–30.

Borko, H. & Livingston, C. (1989). Cognition and improvisation: Differences in mathematics instruction by expert and novice teachers. *American Educational Research Journal 26*(4), 473–498.

Brophy, J. (2000). *Teaching educational practices series–1.* Geneva, Switzerland: International Bureau of Education. (ED 440 066)

Brown, D. F. (2003). Urban teachers' use of culturally responsive management techniques. *Theory into Practice, 42*(4), 277–282.

Bryson, J. M. (1995). *Strategic planning for public and nonprofit organizations: A guide to strengthening and sustaining organizational achievement* (2nd ed.). San Francisco, CA: Jossey-Bass.

Burden, P. R., & Byrd, D. M. (1994). *Methods for effective teaching.* Boston, MA: Allyn and Bacon.

Camphire, G. (2001). Are our teachers good enough? *SEDLetter, 13*(2). Retrieved from http://www.sedl.org/pubs/sedletter/v13n02/1.htm

Carey, K. (2004). The real value of teachers: Using new information about teacher effectiveness to close the achievement gap. *The Education Trust, 8*(1), 5.

Carlisle, E., Stanley, L, & Kemple, K. M. (2005). Opening doors: Understanding school and family influences on family involvement. *Early Childhood Education Journal, 33*(3), 155–162.

Cassidy, W., & Bates, A. (2005). "Drop-outs" and "push-outs": Finding hope at a school that actualizes the ethic of care. *American Journal of Education, 112*(1), 66–102.

Chubbock, S. M., Clift, R. T., Allard, J., & Quinlan, J. (2001). Playing it safe as a novice teacher: Implications for programs for new teachers. *Journal of Teacher Education, 52*(5), 365–376.

Colangelo, N., Assouline, S. G., & Lupkowski-Shoplik, A. E. (2004). Whole-grade acceleration. In N. Colangelo, S. G. Assouline, & M. U. M. Gross (Eds.), *A nation deceived: How schools hold back America's brightest students: The Templeton national report on acceleration* (Vol. 2, pp. 77–86). Iowa City, IA: The Connie Belin & Jacqueline N. Blank International Center for Gifted Education and Talent Development.

Coalition for Psychology in Schools and Education. (2006). *Report on the teacher needs survey.* Washington, DC: American Psychological Association, Center for Psychology in Schools and Education. Retrieved from www. apa.org/ed/cpse/tns_execsummary.pdf

Collinson, V., Killeavy, M., & Stephenson, H. J. (1999). Exemplary teachers: Practicing an ethic of care in England, Ireland, and the United States. *Journal for a Just and Caring Education, 5*(4), 349–366.

Conroy, M. A., Sutherland, K. S., Snyder, A. L., & Marsh, S. (2008). Classwide interventions: Effective instruction makes a difference. *Teaching Exceptional Children, 40*(6), 24–30.

Corbett, D, & Wilson, B. (2004). What urban students say about good teaching. *Educational Leadership, 60*(1), 18–22.

Cotton, K. (1989). Expectations and student outcomes. *School Improvement Research Series, Close Up #7.* Retrieved from http://www.nwrel.org/archive/sirs/4/cu7.html

Cotton, K. (2000). *Research you can use to improve results.* Portland, OR: Northwest Regional Educational Laboratory.

Cotton, K. (2001). Classroom questioning. *School Improvement Research Series, #5.* Retrieved on January 5, 2005, from www.nwrel.scpd/sirs/3/cu5.html

Covino, E. A., & Iwanicki, E. (1996). Experienced teachers: Their constructs on effective teaching. *Journal of Personnel Evaluation in Education, 11,* 325–363.

Cox, J., Daniel, N., & Boston, B. A. (1985). *Educating able learners: Programs and promising practices.* Austin, TX: University of Texas Press.

Crabtree, S. (2004). Teachers who care get most from kids. *The Detroit News.* Retrieved from www.detnews.com/2004/schools/0406/04/a09-173712.htm

Cross, C., & Regden, D. W. (2002). Improving teacher quality. *American School Board Journal asbj.com.* Retrieved from http://www.absj.com/current/coverstory2.html

Cruickshank, D. R., & Haefele, D. (2001). Good teachers, plural. *Educational Leadership, 58*(5), 26–30.

Csikszentmihalyi, M., Rathunde, K., & Whalen, S. (1993). *Talented teenagers: The roots of success and failure.* New York, NY: Cambridge University Press.

Cushing, K. S., Sabers, D. S., & Berliner, D. C. (1992). Olympic gold: Investigation of expertise in teaching. *Educational Horizons, 70*(3), 108–114.

Danielson, C. (1996). *Enhancing professional practice: A framework for teaching.* Alexandria, VA: Association for Supervision and Curriculum Development.

Darling-Hammond, L. (1997). *Doing What matters most: Investing in quality teaching.* New York, NY: National Commission on Teaching and America's Future Teacher's college, Columbia University.

Darling-Hammond, L. (2000). Teacher quality and student achievement: A review of state policy evidence. *Educational Policy Analysis Archive, 8* (1). Retrieved March 21, 2000, from http://olam.ed.asu.edu/epaa/v8n1

Darling-Hammond. (2008). *Powerful learning: What we know about teaching for understanding.* San Francisco, CA: Jossey-Bass.

Darling-Hammond, L., Berry, B., & Thoreson, A. (2001). Does teacher certification matter? Evaluating the evidence. *Educational Policy Analysis, 22*(1), 52–57.

DeCusati, C. L., & Johnson, J. E. (2004). Parents as classroom volunteers and kindergarten students' emergent reading skills. *The Journal of Educational Research, 97*(5), 235–245.

Deslandes, R., & Bertrand, R. (2005). Motivation of parent involvement in secondary-level schooling. *The Journal of Educational Research, 98*(3), 164–175.

Doyle, W. (1986). Classroom organization and management. In M. C. Wittrock (Ed.), *Handbook of research on teaching* (3rd ed., pp. 392–431). New York, NY: Macmillan.

EGMTL Center Curriculum. (n.d.). *Teacher planning and decision making.* Retrieved on June 3, 2005, from http://www2.potsdam.edu/campbemr/egmtlwork/curriculum/college-methods/planning/planning-1.html

Ehrenberg, R. G., & Brewer, D. J. (1995). Did teachers' verbal ability and race matter in the 1960s? Coleman revisited. *Economics of Educational Review, 14*(1), 1–21.

Emmer, E. T., Evertson, C. M., & Anderson, L. M. (1980). Effective classroom management at the beginning of the school year. *The Elementary School Journal, 80*(5), 219–231.

Emmer, E. T., Evertson, C. M., & Worsham, M. E. (2006). *Classroom management for middle and high school teachers* (7th ed.). Boston, MA: Allyn and Bacon.

Engel, D.E. (1994). School leavers in American society: Interviews with school dropouts/stopouts. In R.C. Morris (Ed.). *Using what we know about at-risk youth* (pp. 3–22). Lancaster, PA: Technomic Publishing.

Enghag, M., & Niedderer, H. (2008). Two dimensions of student ownership of learning during small-group work in physics. *International Journal of Science and Mathematics Education, 6,* 629–653.

Ensher, E. A., Heum, C., & Blanchard, A. (2003). Online mentoring and computer-mediated communication: New directions in research. *Journal of Vocational Behavior, 63*(2), 264–288.

Evertson, C. M., Emmer, E. T., & Worsham, M. E. (2006). *Classroom management for elementary teachers* (7th ed.). Boston, MA: Allyn and Bacon.

Farling, M. L., Stone, A. G., & Winston, B. E. (1999). Servant leadership: Setting the stage for empirical research. *The Journal of Leadership Studies, 6*(1/2), 49–72;

Fedestin, B. (2005). When bad teachers happen to good students. *Edutopia, 1*(3), 58.

Felter, M. (1999). High school staff characteristics and mathematics test results. *Educational Policy Analysis Archives, 7*(9). Retrieved December 5, 2000, from http://2paa.asu.edu/epaa/v7n9.html

Ferguson, R.F. (2002). *What doesn't meet the eye: Understanding and addressing racial disparities in high-achieving suburban schools.* Cambridge, MA: Harvard University Press.

Ferguson, P. & Womack, S. T. (1993). The impact of subject matter and education coursework on teaching performance. *Journal of Teacher Education, 44*(1), 55–63.

Fairbanks, S., Simonsen, B., & Sugai, G. (2008). Classwide secondary and tertiary tier practices and systems. *Teaching Exceptional Children 40*(6), 44–52.

Fidler, P. (2002). *The relationship between teacher instructional techniques and characteristics and student achievement in reduced class size classes.* Los Angeles, CA: Los Angeles Unified School District. (ED 473 460).

Fletcher, S. H., & Barrett, A. (2004). Developing effective beginning teachers through mentor-based induction. *Mentoring & Tutoring: Partnership in Learning, 12*(3), 321–333.

Floden, R., & Meniketti, M. (2005). Research on the effects of coursework in the arts and sciences and in the foundations of education. In M. Cochran & K. M. Zeichner (Ed.), *Studying teacher education: The report of the AERA panel on research and panel education* (pp. 261–308). Washington, DC: American Educational Research Association.

Foorman, B. R., Schatschneider, C., Eakin, M. N., Fletcher, J. M., Moats, L. C., & Francis, D. J. (2006). The impact of instructional practices in grades 1 and 2 on reading and spelling achievement in high poverty schools. *Contemporary Educational Psychology, 31*, 1–29. Retrieved from www.sciencedirect.com

Ford, D.Y, & Trotman, M.F. (2001). Teachers of gifted students: Suggested multicultural characteristics and competences. *Roeper Review, 23*(4), 235–239.

Fries, K., & Cochran-Smith, M. (2006). Teacher research and classroom management: What questions do teachers ask? In C. M. Evertson & C. S. Weinstein (Eds.), *Handbook of classroom management: Research, practice, and contemporary issues* (pp. 946–981). Mahwah, NJ: Lawrence Erlbaum Associates.

Fuchs, L. S., Fuchs, D., & Phillips, N. (1994). The relation between teachers' beliefs of the importance of good student work habits, teacher planning, and student achievement. *The Elementary School Journal, 94*(3), 331–345.

Gale, T., & Cosgrove, D. (2004). "We learnt that last week": Reading into the language practices of teachers. *Teachers and Teaching: Theory and Practice, 10*(2), 125–134.

Gannon, J. (2004). A teacher's rules. *Responsive Classroom* website. Retrieved January 2, 2006 from http://www.responsiveclassroom.org/PDF_files/feature_38.asp

Gareis, C. R. (2005, July). *Fighting the "rising tide" of the de-professionalization of teaching: The Clinical Faculty Program at The College of William and Mary.* Presented at the annual conference of the Consortium for Research in Education and Teacher Evaluation, Memphis, TN.

Gareis, C. R., & Grant, L. W. (2008). *Teacher-made assessments: How to connect curriculum, instruction, and student learning.* Larchmont, NY: Eye On Education.

Gettinger, M., & Kohler, K. M. (2006). Process-outcome approaches to classroom management and effective teaching. In C. M. Evertson & C. S. Weinstein (Eds.). *Handbook of classroom management: Research, practice, and contemporary issues* (pp. 73–95). Mahwah, NJ: Lawrence Erlbaum Associates.

Glass, G. V. (2002). Teacher characteristics. In A. Molnar (Ed.), *School reform proposals: The research evidence.* Retrieved on October 25, 2009 from http://epsl.asu.edu/epru/epru_2002_Research_Writing.htm#Writing

Gitomer, D. H., Latham, A. S., & Ziomek, R. (1999). *The academic quality of prospective teachers: The impact of admissions and licensure testing.* Available at http://www.ets.org/Media/Research/pdf/RR-03-35.pdf

Goldhaber, D. D. & Brewer, D. J. (2000). Does teacher certification matter? High school teacher certification status and student achievement. *Educational Evaluation and Policy Analysis, 22*(2), 129–145.

Good, L. (2005). Snap it up: Using digital photography in early childhood. *Childhood Education, 82*(2), 79–85. Retrieved from http://find.galegroup.com.proxy.wm.edu/itx/infomark

Good, T. L., & Brophy, J. E. (1997). *Looking in classrooms* (7th ed.) New York, NY: Addison-Wesley.

Grossman, P., Valencia, S., Evans, K., Thompson, C., Martin, S., & Place, N. (2000). *Transitions into teaching: Learning to teach writing in teacher education and beyond.* Albany, NY: National Research Center on English Teaching and Achievement. (ERIC Document Reproduction Service No. ED 439430).

Halsey, P. A. (2005). Parent involvement in junior high schools: A failure to communicate. *American Secondary Education, 34*(1), 57–69.

Hammerness, K. (2003). Learning to hope, or hoping to learn. *Journal of Teacher Education, 54*(1), 43–56.

Harris, S. (2003). An andragogical model: Learning through life experiences. *Kappa Delta Pi Record, 40*(1), 38–41.

Hattie, J. (2003, October). *Teachers make a difference: What is the research evidence?* Background paper to invited address presented at the 2003 ACER Research Conference, Melbourne, Australia. Retrieved from http://www.acer.edu.au/documents/RC2003_Hattie_TeachersMakeADifference.pdf

Hawk, P. P., Coble, C. R., & Swanson, M. (1985). Certification: Does it matter? *Journal of Teacher Education, 36*(3), 13–15.

Haycock, K. (2000). No more settling for less. *Thinking K-16, 4*(1), 3–12.

Heck, D. J., Banilower, E. R., Weiss, I. R., Rosenberg, S. L. (2008). Studying the effects of professinal development" The case of the NSF's local systemic change through teacher enhancement initiative. *Journal for Research in Mathematics Education, 39*(2), 113–152.

Hindman, J., Stronge, J., & Tucker, P. (2003). Raising the bar: Expecting and getting the best from your students. *Virginia Journal of Education, 97*(3), 7–10.

Hoffman-Kipp, P., Artiles, A. J., & López-Torres, L. (2003). Beyond reflection: Teacher learning as praxis. *Theory into Practice, 42*(3), 244–254, 264.

Hong, B., & Shull, P. (2009, April). Impact of Teacher Dispositions on Student Self-determination. *International Journal of Learning, 16*(1), 261–271.

Hoy, A. W. (2002, October). *The Context for Instructional Leadership.* Presentation for the College of William and Mary Leadership Preparation for Collaborative Service Delivery Project, Williamsburg, VA.

Hoy, A. W., & Hoy, W. K. (2003). *Instructional leadership: A learning-centered guide.* Boston, MA: Allyn & Bacon.

Hoy, A. W., & Weinstein, C. S. (2006). Student and teacher perspectives on classroom management. In C. M. Evertson & C. S. Weinstein (Eds.), *Handbook of classroom management: Research, practice, and contemporary issues* (pp. 181–219). Mahwah, NJ: Lawrence Erlbaum Associates.

Ilmer, S., Snyder, J. Erbaugh, S. & Kurtz, K. (1997). Urban educators' perceptions of successful teaching. *Journal of Teacher Education, 48*(2), 379–384.

Johnson, B. L. (1997). An organizational analysis of multiple perspectives of effective teaching: Implications for teacher evaluation. *Journal of Personnel Evaluation in Education, 11,* 69–87.

Karsenti, T. P. & Thibert, G. (1998, April). *The interaction between teaching practices and the change in motivation of elementary-school children.* Paper presented at the annual meeting of the American Educational Research Association, San Diego, CA. (ERIC Document Reproduction Service No. ED 420397).

Kentish, B. (1995). Hypotheticals: Deepening the understanding of environmental issues through ownership of learning [electronic version]. *Australian Science Teachers Journal, 41*(1), 21–25.

Kinach, B. M. (2002). A cognitive strategy for developing pedagogical content knowledge in the secondary mathematics methods course: Toward a model of effective practice. *Teaching and Teacher Education, 18,* 51–71.

Klecka, C. L, Cheng, Y., & Clift, R. T. (2004). Exploring the potential of electronic mentoring. *Action in Teacher Education, 26*(3), 2–9.

Kohn, A. (1996). What to look for in a classroom. *Educational Leadership, (54)*1, 54–55.

Krüger, M., Witziers, B., & Sleegers, P. (2007). The impact of school leadership on school level factors: Validation of a causal model. *School Effectiveness & Improvement, 18*(1), 1–20. Retrieved from doi:10.1080/09243450600797638

Laczko-Kerr, I., & Berliner, D. C. (2002, September 6). The effectiveness of "Teach for America" and other under-certified teachers on student academic achievement: A case of harmful public policy. *Education Policy Analysis Archives, 10*(37). Retrieved November 4, 2003, from http://epaa.asu.edu/epaa/v10n37/

Leinhart, G. & Greeno, G. H. (1986). The cognitive skill of teaching. *Journal of Educational Psychology, 78*(2), 75–95.

Leithwood, K., Louis, K. S., Anderson, S., & Wahlstrom, K. (2004). *How leadership influences student learning.* Learning From Research Project. Retrieved from http://www.wallace foundation.org/SiteCollectionDocuments/WF/Knowledge%20Center/Attachments/PDF/ReviewofResearch-LearningFromLeadership.pdf

Lewis, R. (2004, October). Helping teachers help students act responsibly. *Proceedings of the Australian Council for Educational Research, Adelaide, South Australia,* 28–33.

Lustick, D., & Sykes, G. (2006). National board certification as professional development: What are teachers learning? *Education Policy Analysis Archives, 14*(5). Retrieved from http://epaa.asu.edu/epaa/v14n5/

Maddux, C. D., Samples-Lachman, I., & Cummings, R.E. (1985). Preferences of gifted students for selected teacher characteristics. *Gifted Child Quarterly, 29*(4), 160–163.

Marzano, R.J. (2003). *What works in schools: Translating research into action.* Alexandria, VA: Association for Supervision and Curriculum Development.

Marzano, R. J., Pickering, D., McTighe, J. (1993). *Assessing student outcomes: Performance assessment using the dimensions of learning model.* Alexandria, VA: Association for Supervision and Curriculum Development.

Mason, D. A., Schroeter, D. D., Combs, R. K., & Washington, K. (1992). Assigning average-achieving eighth graders to advanced mathematics classes in an urban junior high. *The Elementary School Journal, 92*(5), 587–599.

Matheson, A. S. & Shriver, M. D. (2005). Training teachers to give effective commands: Effects on student compliance and academic behaviors. *School Psychology Review, 34*(2), 202–220.

McBer, H. (2000). *Research into teacher effectiveness: A model of teacher effectiveness.* (Research Report #216). London, UK: Department for Education and Employment.

McGavin, H. (2006, February 24). David Lammy—My best teacher. *The Times Educational Supplement.* Retrieved from www.davidlammy.co.uk/da/32019

McLeod, J., Fisher, J., & Hoover, G. (2003). *The key elements of classroom management: Managing time and space, student behavior, and instructional strategies.* Alexandria, VA: Association for Supervision and Curriculum Development.

Meehan, M. L., Cowley, K. S., Schumacher, D., Hauser, B., & Croom, N. D. M. (2003). *Classroom environment, instructional resources, and teaching differences in high-performing Kentucky schools with achievement gaps.* Charleston, WV: AEL. (ERIC Document ED 478 672)

Mendro, R. L. (1998). Student achievement and school and teacher accountability. *Journal of Personnel Evaluation in Education, 12,* 257–267.

Michelson, W., & Harvey, A. S. (2000*). Is teachers' work never done?: Time-use and subjective outcomes.* Retrieved from http://radicalpedagogy.icaap.org/content/issue2_1/02Michelson.html

Miller, J. E., McKenna, M. C., & McKenna, B. A. (1998). A comparison of alternatively and traditionally prepared teachers. *Journal of Teacher Education, 49*(3), 165–176.

Monk, D. H. (1994). Subject area preparation of secondary mathematics and science teachers and student achievement. *Economics of Education Review, 13*(2), 125–145.

Murdock, T. B., & Miller, A. (2003). Teachers as sources of middle school students' motivational identity: Variable-centered and person-centered analytic approaches. *The Elementary School Journal, 103*(4), 383–399.

National Association of Secondary School Principals. (1997). Students say: What makes a good teacher? *NASSP Bulletin, 3,* 15–17.

Naylor, C. (2001). *Teacher workload and stress: An international perspective on human costs and systematic failure.* Vancover, BC: B.C. Teachers' Federation. Retrieved from www.bctf.ca/researchreports/2001wlcol/report.pdf

Nielson, D. C., Barry, A. L., & Addison, A. B. (2006). A model of a new-teacher induction program and teacher perceptions of beneficial components. *Action in Teacher Education, 28*(4), 14–24.

Nikitina, L., & Furuoka, F. (2009, June). Teacher-student relationship and the conceptualization of the good language teacher: Does culture matter? *Asian EFL Journal, 11*(2), 163–187.

Nye, B., Konstantopoulos, S., & Hedges, L. V. (2004). How large are teacher effects? *Educational Evaluation and Policy Analysis, 26*(3), 237–257.

O'Brien, R. C. (2001). *Trust: Releasing the energy to succeed.* New York, NY: John Wiley & Sons.

Occupational Outlook Handbook, 2008–09 Edition, Teachers—Preschool, Kindergarten, Elementary, Middle, and Secondary. Retrieved from http://www.bls.gov/oco/ocos069.htm

Panasuk, R. M., & Sullivan, M. M. (1998). Need for lesson analysis in effective lesson planning. *Education, 118*(3), 330–345.

Patrick, H., Anderman, L. H., Ryan, A. M., Edelin, K. C., & Midgley, C. (2001). Teachers' communication of goal orientations in four fifth grade classrooms. *The Elementary School Journal, 102*(1), 35–58.

Pavlou, V. (2004). Profiling primary school teachers in relation to art teaching. *Journal of Art and Design Education, 23*(1), 35–47.

Peart, N. A., & Campbell, F. A. (1999). At-risk students' perceptions of teacher effectiveness. *Journal for a Just and Caring Education, 5*(3), 269–284.

Peery, A. B. (2004). *Deep change: Professional development from the inside out.* Lanham, MD: Scarecrow Education.

Pitton, D. E. (2006). *Mentoring novice teachers: Fostering a dialogue process* (2nd ed.) Thousand Oaks, CA: Corwin.

Platz, D. L. (1994). Student directed planning: Fostering student ownership in learning. *Education, 114*(3), 420–423.

Pogue, L. L., & AhYun, K. (2006). The effect of teacher nonverbal immediacy and credibility on student motivation and affective learning. *Communication Education, 55*(3), 331–345.

Portner, H. (2003). *Mentoring new teachers.* Thousand Oaks, CA: Corwin

Pressley, M., Raphael, L., Gallagher, J. D., & DiBella, J. (2004). Providence St. Mel school: How a school that works for African American students works. *Journal of Educational Psychology, 96*(2), 216–235.

Prisoners of Time. (1994). Denver, CO: Education Commission of the States. Retrieved from http://eric.edu.gov/ERICWebPortal/

Prusak, K. A., Vincent, S. D., & Pangrazi, R. P. (2005). Teacher talk. *Journal of Physical Education, Recreation,& Dance, 76*(5), 21–25.

Ralph, E. (1998). *Developing practitioners: A handbook of contextual supervision.* Stillwater, OK: New Forums Press.

Ralph, E. G., Kesten, C., Lang, H., & Smith, D. (1998). Hiring new teachers: What do school districts look for? *Journal of Teacher Education, 49*(1), 47–56.

Reynolds, A. (1992). What is competent beginning teaching? A review of the literature. *Review of Educational Research, 62*(1), 1–35.

Robinson, R. (2007). The role of communication in student achievement. *Academic Exchange Quarterly, 11*(2), 21–26.

Rogers, M. P., Abell, S., Lannin, J., Wang, C., Musikul, K., Barker, D., & Dingman, S. (2007). Effective professional development in science and mathematics education: Teachers' and facilitators' views. *International Journal of Science and Mathematics Education, 5,* 507–532.

Rosenthal, R., & Jacobson, L. (1968). *Pygmalion in the classroom.* New York, NY: Holt, Rinehart & Winston.

Ross, J. A., Cousins, J. B., Gadalla, T., & Hannay, L. (1999). Administrative assignment of teachers in restructuring secondary schools: The effect of out-of-field course responsibility on teacher efficacy. *Educational Administration Quarterly, 35,* 782–804.

Rowan, B., Chiang, F. S., & Miller, R. J. (1997). Using research on employees' performance to study the effects of teachers on student achievement. *Sociology of Education, 70,* 256–284.

Rowe, K. (2004, August). *The importance of teaching: Ensuring better schooling by building teacher capacities that maximize the quality of teaching and learning provision—implications from the international and Australian evidence-based research.* Background paper to invited address presented at the Making Schools Better Conference, Melbourne, Australia. Retrieved from http://research.acer.edu.au/learning_processes/14/

Rowe, M. B. (1972). *Wait time and rewards as instructional variables, their influence in language, logic, and fate control.* Chicago, IL: National Association for Research in Science Teaching. (ERIC ED 061103).

Rudney, G. L., & Guillaume, A. M. (2003). *Maximum mentoring: An action guide for teacher trainers and cooperating teachers.* Thousand Oaks, CA: Corwin.

Sabers, D. S., Cushing, K. S., & Berliner, D. C. (1991). Differences among teachers in a task characterized by simultaneity, multidimensionality, and immediacy. *American Educational Research Journal, 28*(1), 63–88.

Sanders, W. L. (2001, January). *The effect of teachers on student achievement.* Keynote address at the Project STARS Institute, Williamsburg, VA.

Scanlon, D., Gelzheiser, L., Vellutino, F., Schatschneider, C., & Sweeney, J. (2008, June). Reducing the incidence of early reading difficulties: Professional Development for classroom teachers versus direct interventions for children. *Learning & Individual Differences, 18*(3), 346–359. Retrieved from doi:10.1016/j.lindif.2008.05.002

Scherer, M. (2001). Improving the quality of the teaching force: A conversation with David C. Berliner. *Educational Leadership, 58*(8), 6–10.

Sharp, K. M. (2003). Teacher reflection: A perspective from the trenches. *Theory into Practice, 42*(3), 243–247.

Shellard, E. & Protheroe, N. (2000). Effective teaching: How do we know it when we see it? *The Informed Educator Series.* Arlington, VA: Educational Research Service.

Singham, M. (2003). The achievement gap: Myths and reality. *Phi Delta Kappan, 84,* 586.

Sleeter, C. E. (2001). Preparing teachers for culturally diverse schools. *Journal of Teacher Education, 52*(2), 94–106.

Smith, T., & Ingersoll, R. (2004). What are the effects of induction and mentoring on beginning teacher turnover? *American Educational Research Journal, 41*(3), 681–714.

Stahl, R. J. (1994). Using "think-time" and "wait-time" skillfully in the classroom. *Eric Digest.* Bloomington, IN: ERIC Clearinghouse for Social Studies/Social Science Education. (ED 370885).

Sternberg, R. E. (2005). Adults who care. *American School Board Journal, 192*(12), 44–47.

Strauss, R. P., & Sawyer, E. A. (1986). Some new evidence on teacher and student competencies. *Economics of Education Review, 5*(1), 41–48.

Stronge, J. H. (2002). *Qualities of effective teachers.* Alexandria, VA: Association for Supervision and Curriculum Development.

Stronge, J. H. (2007). *Qualities of effective teachers* (2nd ed.). Alexandria, VA: Association for Supervision and Curriculum Development.

Stronge, J. H., Gareis, C. R., & Little, C. A. (2006). *Teacher pay and teacher quality: Attracting, developing, and retaining the best.* Thousand Oaks, CA: Corwin.

Stronge, J. H., & Grant, L. W. (2009). *Student Achievement Goal Setting: Using Data to Improve Teaching and Learning*: Larchmont, NY: Eye On Education.

Stronge, J. H., Richard, H. B., & Catano, N. (2008). Qualities of effective principals. Alexandria, VA: Association for Supervision and Curriculum Development.

Stronge, J. H., Tucker, P. D., & Hindman, J. L. (2004). *Handbook for qualities of effective teachers.* Alexandria, VA: Association for Supervision and Curriculum Development.

Stronge, J. H., Tucker, P. D., & Ward, T. J. (2003, April). *Teacher effectiveness and student learning: What do good teachers do?* American Educational Research Association Annual Meeting, Chicago, IL.

Stronge, J. H., Ward, T. J., & Grant, L. W. (2009). *Teacher quality and student learning: What do good teachers do?* (Under review)

Stronge, J. H., Ward, T. J., Tucker, P. D., & Hindman, J. L. (2008). What is the relationship between teacher quality and student achievement? An exploratory study. *Journal of Personnel Evaluation in Education, 20*(3–4), 165–184.

Stronge, J. H., Ward, T. J., Tucker, P. D., Hindman, J. L., McClosky, W., & Howard, B. (2008). National board certified teachers and non-national board certified teachers: Is there a difference in teacher effectiveness and student achievement? *Journal of Personnel Evaluation in Education, 20*(3–4), 185–210.

Supovitz, J. A. (2000). Translating teaching practice into improved student achievement. In S. H. Fuhrman (Ed.), *From the capitol to the classroom: Standards-based reform in the states.* Chicago, IL: University of Chicago Press.

Swope, S. (2004, December 20). A lesser form of immortality? It'll do. *Newsweek, 145*(25), 18.

Swinson, J., & Harrop, A. (2005). An examination of the effects of a short course aimed at enabling teachers in infant, junior and secondary schools to alter the verbal feedback given to their pupils. *Educational Studies 31*(2), 115–30.

Tauber, R. T. (1998). *Good or bad, what teachers expect from students they generally get.* Washington, DC: ERIC Clearinghouse on Teaching and Teacher Education.

The Best Teacher Ever. (n.d.). Retrieved March 23, 2007, from http://www.etni.org.il/bestteacherever.htm

The Way We See It. (2004). Available from http://www.listenup.org

Taylor, R. L., & Wasicsko, M. M. (2000). The disposition to teach. Retrieved October 17, 2003, from www.education.eku.edu/Dean/The Dispositions to Teach.pdf

Telese, J. A. (2008, November). *Teacher professional development in mathematics and student Achievement: A NAEP 2005 Analysis.* Annual Meeting of the School Science and Mathematics Association, Raleigh, NC. Retrieved from http://www.eric.ed.gov. (ED503261).

Thiede, J. (2002). A far cry from business as usual in room 7. *Leadership, 32*(2), 10–11.

Thwaite, A., & Rivalland, J. (2009). How can analysis of classroom talk help teachers reflect on their practices?. *Australian Journal of Language & Literacy, 32*(1), 38–54.

Thweatt, K. S. & McCroskey, J. C. (1998). The impact of teacher immediacy and misbehaviors on teacher credibility. *Communication Education, 47*(4), 348–358.

Treven, J. J., & Hanson, T. L. (2004). The impact of teacher immediacy and perceived caring on teacher competence and trustworthiness. *Communication Quarterly, 51*(1), 39–53.

Tschannen-Moran, M. (2004). *Trust matters: Leadership for successful schools.* San Francisco, CA: Jossey-Bass.

Tucker, P. D., & Stronge, J. H. (2005). *Linking teacher evaluation and student learning.* Alexandria, VA: Association for Supervision and Curriculum Development.

vanDuijenvoorde, A. C., Zanolie, K., Rombouts, A. R., Raijamerks, M. E., & Crone, E. A. (2008). Evaluating the negative or valuing the positive? Neural mechanisms supporting feedback-based learning across development. *The Journal of Neuroscience, 28*(38), 9495–9503.

VanTassel-Baska, J., & Stambaugh, T. (2005). Challenges and possibilities for serving gifted learners in the regular classroom. *Theory into Practice, 44*(3), 211–217.

Van Voorhis, F. L. (2003). Interactive homework in middle school: Effects on family involvement and science achievement. *The Journal of Educational Research, 96*(6), 323–338.

Walker, C. O., & Greene, B. A. (2009). The relations between student motivational beliefs and cognitive engagement in high school. *The Journal of Educational Research, 102*(6), 463–471.

Wallace, M. R. (2009). Making sense of the links: Professional development, teacher practices, and student achievement. *Teachers College Record, 111*(2), 573–596.

Wang, M., Haertel, G.D., & Walberg, H. (1993). Toward a knowledge base for school learning. *Review of Educational Research, 63*(3), 249–294.

Wang, M., Haertel, G. D., & Walberg, H. (1993). What helps students learn? *Educational Leadership, 51*(4), 74.

Weinstein, C., Curran, M. & Tomlinson-Clarke, S. (2003). Culturally responsive classroom management: Awareness into action. *Theory into Practice, 42*(4), 269–276.

Wenglinsky, H. (2000). *How teaching matters: Bringing the classroom back into discussions of teacher quality.* Princeton, NJ: Milliken Family Foundation.

Wenglinsky, H. (2002). How schools matter: The link between teacher classroom practices and student academic performance. *Educational Policy Analysis Archives, 10*(12). Retrieved February 28, 2002 from http://epaa.asu.edu/epaa/v10n12/

Wentzel, K. R. (1997). Student motivation in middle school: The role of perceived pedagogical caring. *Journal of Educational Psychology, 89*(3), 411–419.

Westerman, D. A. (1991). Expert and novice teacher decision making. *Journal of Teacher Education, 42*(4), 292–305.

Whalen, S. P. (1998). Flow and the engagement of talent: Implications for secondary schooling. *NASSP Bulletin, 82*(595), 22–37.

Williams, C. & Forehand, R. (1984). An examination of predictor variables for child compliance and noncompliance. *Journal of Abnormal Psychology, 12*, 491–504.

Wilson, B., Ireton, E., & Wood, J. (1997). Beginning teacher fears. *Education, 117*(3), 380, 396–400.

Wong, H. K., & Wong, R. T. (1998). *The first days of school: How to be an effective teacher.* Mountain View, CA: Harry W. Wong.

Wright, S. P., Horn, S. P., & Sanders, W. L. (1997). Teacher and classroom context effects on student achievement: Implications for teacher evaluation. *Journal of Personnel Evaluation in Education, 11*, 57–67.

Yin, C. C., & Kwok, T. T. (1999). Multimodels of teacher effectiveness: Implications for research. *The Journal of Educational Research, 92*(3), 141–158.

Younger, M. & Warrington, M. (1999). He's such a nice man, but he's so boring, you have to really make an effort to learn: The views of Gemma, Daniel, and their contemporaries on teacher quality and effectiveness. *Educational Review, 51*, 231–241.

Zahorik, J., Halbach, A., Ehrle, K., & Molnar, A. (2003). Teaching practices for smaller classes. *Educational Leadership, 61*(1), 75–77.

Zeichner, K.M. (2003). Pedagogy, knowledge, and teacher preparation. In B. Williams (Ed.), *Closing the achievement gap: A vision for changing beliefs and practices.* (pp. 99–114). Alexandria, VA: Association for Supervision and Curriculum.

Printed and bound by CPI Group (UK) Ltd, Croydon, CR0 4YY

08/06/2025

01896981-0009